KING INK

Nick Cave

King Ink

Nick Cave

FIFTH PRINTING

King Ink first published by:

BLACK SPRING PRESS, Ltd.
126 Cornwall Rd.
London SE1 8TQ
UNITED KINGDOM

Design: **ENDLESS** ∞
Original Black Spring Press edition designed by Phil Baines

Nick Cave and The Bad Seeds recordings are available on Mute Records.
Birthday Party compact discs are available on 2.13.61 Records.

'A Dead Song', 'Dead Joe', 'Truck Love', 'Kiss Me Black' and 'From Her To Eternity'
by Nick Cave and Anita Lane.

'Gun Play #3', 'Emergency Ward. 11:45 P.M.', 'Maine Kelly' and 'Garbage Hearts'
by Nick Cave with Lydia Lunch.

'Wings Off Flies' by Nick Cave with Peter Sutcliffe.

"And I only am escaped to tell thee" – Job

CONTENTS

PRAYERS ON FIRE

Mr Clarinet
Happy Birthday

Prayers on Fire

Zoo Music Girl
Cry
Nick the Stripper
Figure of Fun
King Ink
A Dead Song
Yard
Just You and Me

Release the Bats

MR CLARINET

I have a friend in you, oh Mr Clarionet
You make me laugh, and then cry like the song of the clarinet.
Marry me, marry me alive O
I put on my coat of trumpets
Will she be there? Is my piccolo on straight?

Her white stockings and red dress that goes
swish, swish swish around her legs of lace
Marry me, marry me alive O

Could you tell her
Would you tell her for me, oh Mr Clarinet
That I love her love her, oh love her
I love her but I cannot wait.

Marry me, marry me alive O
Oh maybe, oh maybe lie down

I love her, love her, love her
Love her love her love her love her

HAPPY BIRTHDAY

It's a very happy day
We are at lots of fun fun fun
And it's ice-cream and jelly
and a punch in the belly.
How much can you throw over the walls?

And see how his face glows
It's a bike! What a surprise.
It's a big bike. What a big surprise.
It's a red bike. What a red surprise.
Oh, what a surprise.

But the best thing there
But the best thing there
Was the wonderful dog chair
Was the beautiful dog chair
That could count right up to ten
It could count right up to ten
It went woof, woof, woof, woof, woof,
woof, woof, woof, woof, woof.

And it's another happy day.
He was born eleven years ago
And this year it's long trousers
and a very smart tie.
Just think in five years he'll be shaving.

And see how his face glows
It's a bike. What a surprise!
It's a samurai sword.
What a metal surprise.
He'll remember this day for the rest of his life.

But the best thing there
But the best thing there
Is that fabulous dog chair
The immaculate dog chair
That could count right up to eleven

It could count right up to eleven.
It went woof, woof, woof, woof, woof, woof,
woof, woof, woof, woof, woof, woof.

But the best thing there
But the best thing there
Was my darling the dog chair
But the rampaging dog chair
That could count right up to eleven
It could count right up to eleven.

And it went round and round the house.

Blue Weeds

Blue, Blue ~~Seeds~~ water ~~sand~~ ground

V1. Bloo-wah Seeds scattered →

~~Along~~ Hand over Hand
in ~~your~~ my tattered Hand Baby land
Babyland

Sad, sad Waters
Wash-a-way these blind paths I have on
Run little a
Sad Waters Sad Waters
Wash-a-way Wash-a-way
all the floating promises
sealed with ~~kisses~~ sadder waters
with kisses a-burning
the promises into our faces
Like a brand hide it
+ ya won't
by altering your expressions
till each one holds a face the other don't understand

Roll that rich, Red Carpet down
+ out ~~Heaven~~ of Heaven
(the gates of)
for I sit in the darkness of my night
where the Beasts creep + flee the tarnished harps of MORNING
+ the ~~silver~~ strings of my day + the terrible song that it sings
RUSTED
About a man in chains + the rivers side
being bound in affliction+ in iron
O my feet are bound in fetters + I am laid in
d...... of trammel +
trap

PRAYERS ON FIRE

This place is Hell to me
With the Devil in my bed
And the Devil in this bottle
And the Devil in my head
I'll meet you in Heaven again
If you wear that dress again
(I'll have one more drink, my friend)
Where my heart is kept on ice
And prayers burst into flames
Prayers on fire.

ZOO-MUSIC GIRL

Zoo-Music Girl Zoo-Music Girl
Our life together is a hollow tooth
Spit out the shells, spit out the shells
You know exactly what I'm talking about
Don't drag the orchestra into this thing
Rattle those sticks, rattle those sticks
The sound is beautiful, it's perfect!
The sound of her young legs in stockings
The rhythm of her walk, it's beautiful
Just let it twist, let it break
Let it buckle, let it bend
I want the noise of my Zoo-Music Girl
Zoo-Music Girl Zoo-Music Girl
My body is a monster driven insane
My Heart is a FISH toasted by flames
I kiss the hem of her skirt
We spend our lives in a box full of dirt
I murder her dress till it hurts
I murder her dress and she loves it
If there is one thing I desire in the world
Is to make love to my Zoo-Music Girl
Zoo-Music Girl Zoo-Music Girl
The sound is beautiful! It's perfect!
I call out her name in the night
Zoo-Music Girl! Zoo-Music Girl!
I call her by her family name
Zoo-Music Girl! Zoo-Music Girl!
Oh! God! Please let me die beneath her fists
Zoo-Music Girl Zoo-Music Girl!
Zoo-Music Girl Zoo-Music Girl!

CRY

When ya walk outa here
When ya walk out
I gotta fill up that space
Or fill up that no-space
I'll fill it up with tears
I'll fill it up with tears
I'll fill it up with tears
I'll fill it up with tears
Cry Cry Cry Cry
Where no fish can swim
Where no fish can swim
Where NO-FISH can swim
Where no-fish can
Cry Cry Cry

When ya slam that door
When that door slams
I gotta fill up that space
An' I'll pack my suitcase
I'll fill it up with clothes
Or fill it up with no-clothes
And I'll pack it up with tears

When ya say goodbye
When ya say goodbye
I'll dig myself a hole
And fill up that space
I'll fill it up with flesh
An' I'll fill it up with no-flesh
I'll fill it up with tears

Fish Swim Cry Fish Crryyy

NICK THE STRIPPER

Nick the Stripper
Hideous to the eye
Hideous to the eye
He's a fat little insect
A fat little insect
And OOOOOOOOOH! here we go again

Nick the Stripper
Dances on all fours
Dances on all fours
He's in his birthday suit
He's in his birthday suit
and OOOOOOOOOH! here we go again

Nick the Stripper
Hideous to the eye
Hideous to the eye
He's a fat little insect
A FUCKED little insect
and OOOOOOOOOH! here we go again
Insect Insect Insect Insect

FIGURE OF FUN

I am a figure of fun
Dead-pan and moribund
All the things I do are better left undone
I am a figure of fun.

And I baked in the sun
I have no luck in Love
I have no luck in anything
I am a figure of fun.

And I'm impressed by everyone
But I impress no-one
It's irritating
I am a figure of fun.

I am a figure of fun
I have money
But money isn't everything to a figure of
Fun fun fun fun fun fun.

KING INK

King Ink strolls into town
He sniffs around

King Ink kicks off his stink-boot
Sand and soot and dust and dirt and
He's much bigger than you think
King Ink
King Ink, wake up, get up
Wake up, up, up, up, up, up
A bug crawls up the wall
King Ink feels like a bug
And he hates his rotten shell
Cha-cha-cha-cha-cha-cha-cha-cha
King Ink, get up, go forth,
Wake up—what's in that room?
Wake up—what's in that house?
Express thyself, say something loudly
AAAAAAAH! What's in that room?
Sand and soot and dust and dirt
King Ink feels like a bug
Swimming in a soup-bowl
Oh! Yer! Oh! Yer! What a wonderful life
FATS Domino on the radio

A DEAD SONG

(This is true)
Mister nothing said forever said
I can sing
Hit it! Make it a dead one
With words like
Blood, soldier, mother
O.K. O.K.
I want to sleep before the end
Which is impolite
Hit it! Make it a dead one
If nothing crops up
I'll give you a ring
You can sing the end
O.K. O.K.
Then I could get
All the little animals out of my room
Hit it! With a broom
O.K. O.K.
Put them in a big white sack
No visitors came
Hit it! WITH WORDS LIKE…
Thou shalt not
The End

YARD

In our yard
How many chickens can we count
On our fingers and toes
On their toes
Sitting on father's HOLE
Sitting on his chest
Crushing rocks of dirt
The earth is soft in our
Yard Yard
Stones in my shoes
And feet
Dragging them through museums
Where
Under glass
Refridgerate
Freeze
Hands and feet
And knobbly knees
Yard Yard

JUST YOU AND ME

First: I tried to kill it with a hammer
Thought that I could lose
The head.
Sure! We've eaten off the silver
(When even food was against us)
And then I tried to kill it in the bed.
Second: I gagged it with a pillow
But awoke the nuns inside
My head.
They pounded their Goddy-Goddy fists
(From the inside – so from the outside)
I got good: I STUCK IT. Dead.
Thirdly: I put my lips upon it
And blew a frost across
Its flat.
I wrote upon its outside-surface
'Tonite we're on the outside-surface'
Just you and me girl: you and me and the fat.

RELEASE THE BATS

Whooah Bite! Whooah Bite!
Release the bats. Release the bats.
Don't tell me that it doesn't hurt
A hundred fluttering in your skirt
(Don't tell me that it doesn't hurt).

My baby is alright
She doesn't mind a bit of dirt
She says 'Horror vampire bat bite'
She says 'Horror vampire
How I wish those bats would bite'
Whoooah Bite! Bite!

Release the bats! Release the bats!
Pump them up and explode the things
Her legs are chafed by sticky wings
(Sticky sticky little things).

My baby is a cool machine
She moves to the pulse of her generator
Says damn that sex supreme.
She says damn that horror bat
Sex vampire, cool machine.

Release the bats! Release the bats!
Release them!

Baby is a cool machine
She moves to the pulse of a generator
She says damn that sex supreme
She says, she says damn that horror bat
Sex horror sex bat sex horror sex vampire
Sex bat horror vampire sex.
Cool machine.
Horror bat. Bite!
Cool machine. Bite!
Sex vampire. Bite!

JUNKYARD

Big-Jesus-Trash-Can
Kiss Me Black
6" Gold Blade
Kewpie Doll
Junkyard
She's Hit
Dead Joe
Hamlet (Pow, Pow, Pow)

Sometimes Pleasure Heads Must Burn

BIG – JESUS – TRASH – CAN

BIG – JESUS soul-mates TRASH – CAN
fucking rotten business this
both feet in the Bad-Boot
stiff in the crypt, babay, like a rock
rock-rock-rock
BIG – JESUS soul-mates TRASH – CAN
pumped me fulla TRASH at least it smelt like TRASH
wears a suit of Gold (got greasy hair)
but god gave me Sex appeal

well-well-well-well-rock
well-well-well-well-rock
well-well-well-well-rock
well-well-well-well-rock
he drives a TRASH – CAN
he drives a TRASH – CAN
he drives a TRASH – CAN
he drives a TRASH – CAN
he's comin' to my town rock-rock-rock-
r-o-o-o-o-o-o-o-o-o-o-o-o-o-o-o-ck !

BIG – JESUS – OIL – King down in Texas
drives great holy tanks of Gold
Screams from heaven's Graveyard
American heads will roll in Texas
    (roll like Daddies' Meat)
roll under those singing stars of Texas

well-well-well-well-rock
well-well-well-well-rock
well-well-well-well-rock
well-well-well-well-rock
he drives a TRASH – CAN
he drives a TRASH – CAN
he drives a TRASH – CAN
he drives a TRASH – CAN
He's comin' to my town, He's comin' to my town
He's comin' to my town, He's comin' to my town.

KISS ME BLACK

NOW THEY put the STINK on us
Throw us to the succubus
Fed us to the incubus
And brung in the Saprophagus
c'mon and kiss me black
I need to feel your lips around me
c'mon and kiss me black
Black as the pit in which you found me.

She's like a dog you have to kick her
Sleeps like a swastika
And says 'everyone's a winner now
cos everyone's a sinner now'
come on and kiss me black
come and sail your ships around me
c'mon and kiss me black
Black as the sea in which you drowned me.

C'mon and kiss me black
Run your rusty cutlass through me
C'mon and kiss me black
Kiss me black and then undo me.

6" GOLD BLADE

I stuck a six-inch gold blade in the head of a girl.
She: lying through her teeth, him: on his back
Hands off this one, hands off! she cried
grinning at me from hip to hip
Hands off, pretty baby, tough bone then so soft to slip
Oooh Yeah.
I stuck a six-inch gold blade in the head of a girl
Sharks-fin slices sugar-bed slices that pretty red-head
I LOVE YOU! now me! I LOVE YOU!
laughter, laughter
Oh baby, those skinny girls, they're so quick to murder
Oooh Yeah
Shake it baby, c'mon, shake, shake it baby ad infinitum

KEWPIE DOLL

WELL I love that kewpie doll
Well I love that kewpie doll
Well I love that kewpie doll
yeah I bought her in a show
I dressed her up in a cheap red cotton dress
but everything was either FISHED–OUT or SPAT–OUT
FISHED–OUT or SPAT–OUT
well I love that kewpie-doll
but I could not make it stick
well I love that kewpie-doll
but I could not make it stick
only she could save my soul
she put her hands inside of me
well I love that kewpie-doll
Dressed her in a cheap-red-cotton-dress
FISHED IT OUT now SPAT IT OUT now
SPAT IT OUT in front of me
Well I love that kewpie-doll
but I could not make it stick
doll doll doll doll doll doll doll doll
I held her in my cheap arms
she believed in me, she believed in me
her soul and my arms
well I love that kewpie-doll
I told her phoney stories
well I love that kewpie-doll
she believed in me
doll doll doll doll doll doll doll doll
kewpie on a stick
I can see her coming even now
kewpie on a stick
I can see her walking to me even now
well I love that kewpie-doll
I can see her walking to me even now
well I love that kewpie-doll
I can see her walking to me even now
well I love that kewpie-doll
but I could not make it stick. end.

JUNKYARD

I am the King. I am the King. I am the King.

One dead marine through the hatch
Scratch and scrape this heavenly body
every inch of winning skin
there's garbage in honey's sack again.

Honey Honey Honey Honey Honey
come on and kiss me-e-e-e-e-e
Honey Honey Honey Honey Honey
Honey-child's takin' over this place.

Two dead marines standing in a line
Drink to me! this heavenly body
Every inch a winning thing.

Honey Honey Honey Honey Honey
come on and kiss me-e-e-e-e-e
Honey Honey Honey Honey Honey
Honey-child's takin' over this place.

hack hack hack hack this heavenly
yack yack yack yack yack goes junk-face
scratch scrape scratch this winning skin
there's garbage in Honey's sack again
there's garbage in Honey's sack again
there's garbage in Honey's sack again
GARBAGE IN HONEY Garbage in Honey
Junkyard King Junkyard King
King King King King King

SHE'S HIT

there is woman-pie in here
mr. evangelist says she's hit
the best cook ya ever had
ya can't blame the good-woman now, dad
and ya locked him up for twenty years
now there's action on the basement stairs
a monster half-man half-beast
hear the hatchet (grind grind)
pilgrim gets 1 hacked daughter
and all we guys get are forty hack reporters
uptown one hundred skirts are bleeding
mr. evangelist says
she's hit ev'ry little bit
she's hit ev'ry little bit
now if only we could all grow wings and fly
sweet hatchet SWING low son
I'm feeling pretty lonesome
christen the bastard jack dad
the head-shrinker is a quack
'anyone who'd wear their hair like that'
the vinyl is so cool/the conversation's cruel
hold my heart romeo it's in a rodeo
hold my head daddy-o it just won't go-o-o-o
and all the girls across the world
and all the girls across the world
are hit ev'ry little bit
goodbye.

DEAD JOE

oh-ho-ho-ho-ho-ho-ho-ho-ho-ho Dead Joe
oh-ho-ho-ho-ho-ho-ho-ho-ho-ho Dead Joe

welcome to the car smash
welcome to the car smash
welcome to the car smash
Dead Joe

Junk-Sculpture turning back to JUNK
Junk-Sculpture turning back to JUNK
Junk-Sculpture turning back to JUNK
Dead Joe
oh joe n-o-o-o-o-o!! it's christmas time Joe
it's christmas time now for you
and all the little bells are hanging two-by-two
the holly and the nativity
oh speak to me Joe speak to me Joe speak to me oh
oh-oh-oh—oh—oh—oh—oh—oh—oh—oh
De-e-e-e-e-e-e-e-e-e-e-e-e-ead Joe

oh-ho-ho-ho-ho-ho-ho-ho-ho-ho Dead Joe!
oh-ho-ho-ho-ho-ho-ho-ho-ho-ho Dead Joe!

welcome to the car smash
welcome to the car smash
welcome to the car smash
you can't tell the girls from the boys anymore
you can't tell the girls from the boys anymore
you can't tell the girls from the boys anymore
ho-Oh-Oh-OH-Oh-Oh—Oh—Oh—Oh—Oh—Oh—Oh
De-e-e-e-e-e-e-e-e-e-e-e-e-ead Joe.

HAMLET (POW, POW, POW)

Hamlet's fishin' in the grave
Hamlet's fishin' in the grave
thru the CUSTARD bones and stuff
he ain't got no friends in there
he ain't got no friends in there
I believe our man's in love
Hamlet got a gun-now
he wears a CRUCIFIX
he wears a CRUCIFIX
pow pow pow pow/pow pow pow pow
Hamlet moves so beautiful
Hamlet moves so beautiful
walking thru the flowers
who are hiding 'round the corners
He's movin' down the street-now
he likes the look of that CADILLAC
he likes the look of that CADILLAC
pow pow pow pow/pow pow pow pow
IS THIS LOVE some kinda love
IS THIS LOVE some kinda love
Now he's movin' down my street
and he's coming to my house
crawling up my stairs
WHEREFORE ART THOU BABY-FACE
Where-for-art-thou
pow pow pow pow/pow pow pow pow
Is this love
Is this love
POW!
He shoot it inside
He shoot it inside
POW !
Don't let 'em steal your heart away
he went and stole my heart POW!!
hey hey hey POW!!

SOMETIMES PLEASURE HEADS MUST BURN

BU-U-U-U-U-U-U-RN! POP! POP!
BU-U-U-U-U-U-U-RN! POP! POP!
I reckon I'm a bit too close to this one
I reckon if I touch it might just burn
Flesh-heads like me just wax and melt
When my tongue touches titty's tongue in turn
Sometimes pleasure heads must
BU-U-U-U-U-U-U-RN! POP! POP!
BU-U-U-U-U-U-U-RN! POP! POP!
My brain tricked my hands to believe they were strong
In short, my hands became clubs to grind
I reckon I'm a bit too close to this one
Kiss me darling, kiss my eyes to blind
Kiss my clubs and witness what my knuckles find
BU-U-U-U-U-U-U-RN! POP! POP!
BU-U-U-U-U-U-U-RN! POP! POP!
I feel a little low, you know what I mean?
Buried neck-high in British snow
I reckon I'm a bit too close to this one
Shoot me darling, shoot me in the head and go
Ya! Ya! Teeth gone. Follow my trail back home.
Ya! Ya! Teeth gone. Follow my trail back home.
Ya! Ya! BU-U-U-U-U-U-U-RN! POP! POP!
Etcetera.

THE BAD SEED

Sonny's Burning
Wild World
Fears of Gun
Deep in the Woods

SONNY'S BURNING

Have you heard how Sonny's burning
Like some bright erotic star?
He lights up the proceedings
And raises the temperature.
Flame on! Flame on!

Now I've seen to Sonny's Burning
Someday I think I'll cut him down
But it can get so cold in here
And he gives off such an evil heat.
Flame on! Flame on!
Hail my incubatic incubator.

Now pay witness to Sonny's Burning
Warming the damp and rotten seed
Warming the damp and rotten seed
That blooms into the DEMON FLOWER
Now fire and flowers both consume me.
Flame on! Flame on!

Evil heat is running through me
Flame on! Flame on!
Sonny's burning pits into me
Flame on! Flame on!
Sonny's burning holes into me
Don't interrupt! Don't interrupt!
Flame on! Flame on!

WILD WORLD

Hold me up baby for I may fall
Hold my dish-rag body tall
Our bodies melt together (we are one)
Post crucifixion baby, and all undone.

It's a wild world

Church bells ring out the toll of our night
Forward and forever backward
Forever backward forever forward alright
Strophe and antistrophe
(C'mon baby, hold me tight)
It's a wild world, a wild world
Up here in your arms tonight.

Don't push me
Don't push me

It's a wild world.

FEARS OF GUN

Gun wears his alcoholism well
Finger in Bottle and swingin' it still
From Bed to Sink and back again
Clock is crawlin' round the same
He's bustin' Clock (he hates its face)
Just sittin' and talkin' to Heart in ticks
Talkin' back to Clock in slow and studied kicks
The fears of Gun are the fears of everyone.

Fingers down the throat of love
Fingers down the throat of love
Fingers down the throat of love
Love! Love!

Gun does the waltz around the room
Collecting Table and Chairs and Sofa and so on and so on
Gun wears his best blue suit, now let's take to the sky
'We'll go dancin' and eatin' it up
Get a bottle and push it on down'
And let's just beat it up
Transistor radio plays an overwhelmingly sad and lonely song
Saying 'Where she gone? Where she gone?'
The fears of Gun are the fears of everyone.

Fingers down the throat of love
Fingers down the throat of love
Love! Love!

DEEP IN THE WOODS

The woods eats the woman and dumps her honey-body in the mud.
Her dress floats down the well and it assumes the shape of the
body of a little girl.

Yeah I recognize that girl
She stumbled in some time last loneliness
But I could not stand to touch her now
My one and onlyness.

Deep in the woods
Deep in the woods
Deep in the woods a funeral is swinging.

Worms make their cruel design
Saying D-I-E into her skin
Saying DEAD into belly and DEATH into shoulder
Well last night she kissed me but than DEATH was upon her.

Deep in the woods
Deep in the woods
Deep in the woods a funeral is swinging.

Now the killed waits for the killer
And the trees all nod their heads, they are agreed
This knife feels like a knife feels like a knife that feels like it's feed.
Yeah I recognize that girl
I took her from rags right through to stitches (pray for me now)
Oh baby, tonight we sleep in separate ditches.

Deep in the woods
Deep in the woods
Deep in the woods a funeral is swinging.

Love is for fools and all fools are lovers
It's raining on my house and none of the others
Love is for fools and God knows I'm still one
The sidewalks are full of love's lonely children
The sidewalk regrets that we had to kill them.

THE DIE HAUT ALBUM

Truck Love
Stow-a-Way
Dumb Europe
Pleasure is the Boss

TRUCK LOVE

Truck love! Right here!
Truck love! Right now!
Bewitched by pure power. That's truck love!
In the gully of your choice. Truck love!
Jam-up on a leaping tree. Head on! Head first!
And God came down and talked to me
And I damn nearly wept.
Tears rolling down the dash! Tears rolling down the dash!
We can't stop the monster rolling
We can't stop the monster rolling
We can't stop the monster rolling
We can't stop the monster rolling
Rise to power! Rise to power!
Rise to power! Rise to power!
Your stare bright like gold
Eye-spot interference all across the fucking road.
Burn my eyes! Burn my eyes! Baybeeeeee!
My hands keep shaking when I'm touching ya
My hands keep shaking when I'm touching ya
They keep shaking when I ain't
They keep shaking when I ain't.

Truck love! Truck love!
Pit-stop lovers!
Right now and the now is right!
This highway is done bent on killing us
Testing every nerve that we possess between us.
The face of Christ is leaping from the storm
The face of Christ is leaping from the storm
You tend to get religious on these runs.
Rise to power! Rise to power!
Rise to power! Rise to power!
Divine power has gone crawled into this tank
Every metal muscle flexed and pumping at the crank.
Pumping at my axis. Rendering me sexless.
Mega-tons of muscle kicking dust across Texas.

Truck love! Out on the city limits
Drive straight into the eye of the next town that we hit
Gun it once for the hillbillys
Just to make them shit.

Fuck love! This truck love!
Fuck love! This truck love!
The dolls on the grill are caked in bloody bug guts
The dolls on the grill are caked in bloody bug guts
Truck love! Truck love!
Rise to power! Rise to power!
The dolls on the grill are caked in bloody bug guts
The dolls on the grill are caked in bloody bug guts
Truck love! Truck love!
There are things burning in the desert
Rise to power! Rise to power!
There are things burning in the desert
Rise to power! Rise to power!
There are things burning in the desert.

STOW-A-WAY

Hey hey I am the stow-a-way
Hey hey I am the stow-a-way

My girl turned as blue as an iceberg do
And me I'm totally shipwrecked over her
Baby baby don't blow away
Hey hey I am the stow-a-way
I am the stow-a-way

This is your captain talking to ya
This is your captain talking to ya
This is your captain talking to ya
This is your captain talking to ya

Heartache

Hey hey I am the stow-a-way
I am the stow-a-way

My baby turned as blue as an iceberg do
And I sank to the bottom of the sea
Hey baby don't blow away
Hey hey I am the stow-a-way
I am the stow-a-way

This is your doctor talking to ya
This is your doctor talking to ya
This is your doctor talking to ya
This is your doctor talking to ya

Heartache

DUMB EUROPE

On this European night out on the brink
The cafes and the bars still stink
The air is much too thick for seeing
But not thick enough for leaning
I leave in a catatonic crawl
And if I die tonight then throw me in
Some bleak teutonic hole
Six feet under with a snap-frozen soul
And really we could all just die of shame
And really we could all just die of shame
Dumb Europe, Dumb Europe, Dumb Europe.

Oh the Utopian night on the brink
Mama's face staring up at me from the bottom of the sink
Witness my trail of destruction
Trying to leave this drinking place
My feet are magnetized for furniture
The floor's attracted to my face
And if I die tonight
Sell me as some prehistoric bone
A lump of junk-souvenir for Jap
To fob off on his friends back home
The money-dance ....
I find it hard to cope with days like this. Pass the bottle etcetera
Dumb Europe, Dumb Europe, Dumb Europe.

On this European night out on the brink
The cafes and the bars still stink
The air is much too thick for seeing
But not thick enough for leaning
I leave in a catatonic crawl
And if I die tonight then throw me in
Some bleak teutonic hole
Six feet under with a snap-frozen soul
And really we could all just die of shame
And really we could all just die of shame
Dumb Europe, Dumb Europe, Dumb Europe.

PLEASURE IS THE BOSS

They're working us like dogs around here
'Cause pleasure is the boss
And I'm the happiest slave alive around here
'Cause pleasure is the boss
And nothing is safe that don't stand still
If it's O.K. with the boss
I'm gunna walk right up and take it yeah
If it's O.K. with the boss.

Walk!

What's O.K. with the boss is O.K. with me
What's O.K. with the boss is O.K. with me

What's O.K. with the boss is O.K. with me
What's O.K. with the boss is O.K. with me

What's O.K. with the boss is O.K. with me
What's O.K. with the boss is O.K. with me.

MUTINY!

Jennifer's Veil
Mutiny in Heaven
Swampland

Vixo

JENNIFER'S VEIL

So you've come back for Jennifer
You know, she hides her face behind a veil
I'm warning you Frankie, leave on the next train
Your Jennifer she just ain't the same
Quit waving that thing about! Come back!
Come back and give me a chance to explain
Your baby will never cry again.

So don't try to reach out
And don't let the ship's flag down
Point the figure-head at the storm
And drive her hard upon
Don't stop and don't stop
And don't let the veil drop
(Another ship ready to sail—the rigging is tight
Tight like Jennifer's veil).

She drew the curtain on her face
Ever since they came and burnt the old place down
Why is she searching through the ashes?
Why, only Jennifer knows that now.
And the officer, without a word,
Left all his junk and just moved out.

So don't try to reach out
And don't let the ship's flag down
Point the figure-head at the glass
Smash! Smash! into shards
Don't stop and don't touch!
And don't let the veil drop… behind Jennifer's veil.

Oh God! Frankie! Is that really you!
Get back! Don't reach out!
Get back, and get that lantern out of my room!

Don't try to reach out
And don't let the ship's flag down
Down, down over her, like a shroud

And let her sail on the sea like a stone.
Don't touch and don't touch
And don't let the veil drop
Another ship ready to dock …the rigging comes loose…

MUTINY IN HEAVEN

Well ah jumpt! and fled this fucken heap on doctored wings
Mah flailin pinions, with splints and rags and crutches!
      (Damn things nearly hardly flap)
Canker upon canker upon one million tiny punctures
                            That look like…
Long thin red ribbons draped across the arms of a lil mortal girl
      (Like a ground-plan of Hell)
Curse these smartin strings! These fucken ruptures!
Enough! Enough is enough!
      (If this is Heaven ah'm bailin out)
If this is Heaven, ah'm bailin out!
Ah caint tolerate this ol tin-tub
So fulla trash and rats! Felt one crawl across mah soul
For a seckon there, ah thought ah wassa back down in the ghetto!
      (Rats in Paradise! Rats in Paradise!)
Ah'm bailin out! There's a mutiny in Heaven!

Ah wassa born…
And Lord shakin, even then was dumpt into some icy font,
                like some great stinky unclean!
From slum-church to slum-church, ah spilt mah heart
To some fat cunt behind a screen…
Evil poppin eye presst up to the opening
He'd slide shut the lil perforated hatch… at night mah body blusht

To the whistle of the birch
With a lil practice ah soon learnt to use it on mahself
Punishment?! Reward!! Punishment?! Reward!!
Well, ah tied on… percht on mah bed ah was…
                sticken a needle in mah arm…
Ah tied off! Fucken wings burst out mah back
      (Like ah was cuttin teeth!!)
Ah took off!!!
      (Rats in Paradise! Rats in Paradise!)
There's a mutiny in Heaven!

Oh Lord, ah git down on mah knees
       (Ah git down on mah knees and start to pray)

Wrapt in mah mongrel wings, ah nearly freeze
In the howlin wind and drivin rain
       (All the trash blowin round 'n' round)
From slum-heaven into town
Ah take mah tiny pain and rollin back mah sleeve
       (Roll anna roll anna roll anna roll)
Ah yank the drip outa mah vein! UTOPIATE! Ah'm bailin out!
                             UTOPIATE!
If this is Heaven ah'm bailin out!
Mah threadbare soul teems with vermin and louse
Thought comes like a plague to the head… in God's house!
Mutiny in Heaven!
       (Ars infectio forco Dio)
To the plank!
       (Rats in Paradise! Rats in Paradise!)
Ah'm bailin out!
       (Hail Hypuss Dermio Vita Rex!)
Hole inna ghetto! Hole inna ghetto!
       (Scabio Murem per Sanctum… Dio, Dio, Dio)

SWAMPLAND

Quixanne, ah'm in its grip
Quixanne, ah'm in its grip
Sinken in the mud
Patron-saint of the Bog.
They cum with boots of blud
Wit pitchfawk and with club
Chantin out mah name
Got doggies strainin onna chain
Lucy, ah'll love ya till the end!
They hunt me like a dog
Down in Sw-a-a-a-amp Land!

So cum mah executioners! Cum bounty hunters!
Cum mah county killers—for ah cannot run no more
Ah cannot run no more
Ah cannot run no more
No I can't!
Lucy, ya won't see this face agin
When ya caught ya swing and burn…
Down in Sw-a-a-a-amp Land!

The trees are veiled in fog
The trees are veiled in fog
Like so many jilted brides
Now they're all breakin down and cry
Cryin tears upon mah face
Cryin tears upon mah face
And they smell of gasolene
a-a-a-a-ah scr-e-e-e-a-m
Lucy, ya made a sinner out of me
Now ah'm burnin like a saint
Down in Sw-a-a-a-amp Land!

So cum mah executioners! Cum mah bounty huntahs!
Cum mah county killers—ya know ah cannot run no more
No ah cannot run no more.

VIXO

Ah fed Vixo on ev'ry fear 'n' fret 'n' phobia
Til it nor ah could stand the strain no longer
Sucked a chicken-bone, tossed it in the corner
Raisin up like Lazarus, up, up from its cot
An making for the door, now…
Infant-prodigy creates a phantom-friend, yeah
Stickin' sack an ol' Jack-Jack into its itchin-ten
Oh! Don't ya linger! Ooh! Don't ya linger, now,
Mah monster-piece… mah perfect-murder-machine
Don't ya linger, for ah can feel mah youth slipping outa me
Yeah, ah can feel mah youth slip outa me.

Call it, Call it Vixo. Call it Vee.
Ah all it, an it comes to me.
Call it Vixo. Call it me
March headlong into the heart of fear
Ah will follow thee.

What kept ya? Whaa? What kept ya? You get trouble? Sum'n go wrong?
Vixo grinning, climbs up into mah lil boy arms.
What you get? Tell me, what ya gone 'n' brung me from the hollow?
Yeah! We're laughin'… but our laughter is shallow
Ain't it funny… my childhood name is Sorrow.
Vixo sighs, 'n' lays its head upon mah pillow.

Call it. Call it Vixo. Call it Vee.
Call it, an it comes to me.
Vee… ah… Hex… Oh-oh, come crawl with me.
Into the dark heart of despair
Ah will not forsake thee.

Listen... Instruction!
Ditch it, Pitch it. Now hitch it up along the ridge
Ya laughin b'neath the Sherriff's wheels
That go screamin cross Hooper Bridge
Skirt the out-skirts. Up mah back-stair. Ya sack all undone.
Don't touch nothin! Water runnin in the tub
Get there! and scrub ev'ry one.

When ya STRUCK ya STRUCK! Ya struck a thousand crickets dumb
Hooper-Hollow iced over then, all hush, hush
In the cool midday sun
Hush! Ah say Hush! Hu-u-u-ush!
Sittin on the roof, laugh at mahself
As they rope off the woods
Watchin' all the good-people
go beating the bush.

SELECTED ONE ACT PLAYS

The Five Fools
Gun Play # 3
Emergency Ward 11:45pm
Maine Kelly (and me on a bender)
Garbage Hearts

Golden–Horn–Hooligan
American–Speedway–Fever–Trash
Greasy–Hot–Rod–Cream
Grease–Gun–Shooter

THE FIVE FOOLS

SCENE

Priest, aged 50, ecclesiastical garb, face a mass of heavy lines. His right hand is missing. He produces a small hatchet which he carefully screws into the attachment on his stump. He spreads a small, slightly soiled cloth upon the table. He bangs his tightly closed fist upon the cloth. He stares at it.

PRIEST: *[tense]* Expose yourselves, cowards. You have sinned against both your master and your God and you will pay the penalty.

> *[He opens his hand, stretching his fingers wide–still he contemplates them.]*

Ah, my wicked friends–my unfortunate five. You really mix with the wrong crowd. Don't think I don't know your little quirks. I understand each of your personal problems. I understand exactly. It's the company you keep–you've corrupted each other. I would have thought you'd learned your lesson, but you've really gone and pushed it too far. No turning back. I set an example with your colleagues. [He rubs his stump at the base of the hatchet.] But you were blind–too absorbed in your own voices. So, listen to me now. . . YOU WILL PAY. There is no room for forgiveness now, my quivering quintet.

> *[He raises the hatchet.]*

BE BRAVE!!

> *[He slams it down, severing the first finger.]*

The first is for GUILT! The pointer–the condemner. You are free–arrogant probe, never to prod me into inescapable corners of guilt again. Never again will I be poked guilty and mean, and be forced to carry all man's blame. Never shall you wag at me as I suffer, never, no never.

[He brings the hatchet down, and with a sickly thud he removes the second finger.]

This is for the school of hard knocks–the vertical beam–the main trunk of the cross–the life support and the big one. Good riddance to your cruel lesson. The devil's lesson of life. Good riddance to life, yes, THE SCHOOL OF HARD KNOCKS–the warmonger and the sick one. I say–go now. Even in death you will haunt me.

[With a terrible grimace he lops off the third]

This is the CROSS BEAM stained crimson with blood of trickery and deceit. It is the holy support. This is the church of stone, fleshless, soulless, and silent. Many times my lips have chilled upon your walls, my feet frozen upon your floors. Be damned, frigid edifice—leave this wretched company.

[Again his arm rises.]

And finally the RUNT.

[And again he brings the hatchet down.]

The last is for DESIRE–squashed, for stunted lust. Excommunicate the runt. Smash the wall between the knife and the flesh. The forces that repress be gone… NOW I CAN INDULGE. NOW I CAN WALLOW.

[He holds his bleeding stump to his face.]

The thumb shall remain, so I can condemn, provide warning, punish, intrude, violate—in short, puncture the O.

[He faints.]

CURTAIN

GUN PLAY # 3

Gaudy coloured lights flood the stage on which a young man spins a blind-folded and female partner around in the background [loud]. She stumbles, squeals w/laughter, stumbles [oh how silly] a bit more and then mouth open and still giggling [arms outstretched] she makes a gay little bee-line toward the young man. When at arms' reach [Is that you, Tommy, giggle] the man jams a Colt 45 into her mouth and blows off the back of her head. The Big O sings 'Pretty Woman'… oh.

BLACKOUT

EMERGENCY WARD 11:45 P.M.

Emergency ward of the Star of Bethlehem hospital on a Saturday night. The clock on the wall says 11:45. Not a bad night. Let's say about fifteen limbs to half a dozen patients. The protagonist. His head wrapped in a bandage from which spurts vast quantities of blood. Sterile white lights illuminate this action for about nine pints. Our hero slumps forward. Nurses pacing every which way, shoes squeaking, buttocks clenched, busy. Very busy.

CURTAIN

MAINE KELLY (AND ME ON A BENDER)

SCENE

The action takes place inside a single carriage, empty but for rotting straw, blow-flies etc., in a graveyard of trains. I [stinking black suit, black, taped-up shades, large misshapen hat] sit drunk, clutching shitty 2 string guitar, reminiscing with two other low lives. I strum for punctuation.

ME: *[Through broken teeth]* Now I wanna tell ya about Maine… Maine Kelly and me on a bender. *[Strums]* He was a big man… Big arms, big hands, big head, and one great big heart. Yeah, we were a couple of do-bads on one helluva bender. Bustin' ass and bustin' heads like he was never going home. Suck-guzzlin' fuckers we was, drinking some cheap shit. *[Strums]* Yeah… I'm gunna tell ya, Maine Kelly was some great fuckin' grizzly… That bastard could fuck every Marilou in town and still save some up for Mama. *[Pause]* Yeah I can tell what you're thinking. I can tell… It was a man's world, man, a man's world… And Sally pumped the beer and Nancy offered ass and come Sunday, after a week of forty days and forty nights, was we fucked to the gills? Pickled rotten? Screwed dickless?? Was we? Why FUCK NO!! Maine Kelly and me was still the two-fisted, shitkicking, steel-gutted, cunt-stuffing, sons of cunts and pretty flowers that we ever was. *[Strum]*.

The two unfortunates rise and kick me black and blue. Smashing guitar along the way…

CURTAIN

GARBAGE HEARTS

SCENE

Up against the garbage dumpster, knee between her legs, he takes deep inhalation. The garbage and her uniform. Putting his prick where his knee was prior, the tip of it comes into contact. The skin collects under her fingernails as he rams it home. The repeated cracks of her skull against the dumpster bang out the rhythm of passion. He dribbles out.

GIRL: *[Pulls away]* I'm late for work and I am a waitress in a truck stop. What about you?

BOY: *[In blue jeans and t-shirt, turns his face to light]* Nothing.

BLACKOUT

GOLDEN–HORN–HOOLIGAN

SCENE

A single spot-light illuminates GOLDEN—HORN—HOOLIGAN who sits on the bonnet of a big-golden-hot-rod-car. He is dressed in a leather jump-suit which is of the deepest inky-blue, which serves to plant the seed of sadness into the hearts of the audience and forewarns of the monstrous tragedy ahead. GOLDEN—HORN—HOOLIGAN stares into space, the weight of the world upon his shoulders. He remains that way for some time then slowly lifts his head.

GOLDEN—HORN—HOOLIGAN: I am Golden-Horn-Hooligan. *[He rolls the words in his mouth]* Golden .... Horn .... Hooligan: ... I've got a girl, best on the track, dark eyes and a sweater saying Golden-Horn-Hooligan and a red dress that goes swish-swish when she walks and I got Pope-Panther, my car, fastest and leanest around and I got a cupboard fulla cups, golden cups that gave me my name and my proud-proud stride and I got cash, yeah, cash to burn and all... all *[softly]*... all. *[He stands up and circles the car]* Ten years I have driven hard I mean real hard around the track, thousands and thousands of times, around and around the circle. In my earliest days the circle seemed so long, the flag would drop and it would seem an eternity till I was doubling my tracks but speed came fast and I learned speed and the circle got smaller and I was winning and taking the cash and my cars got better and then I got Pope-Panther the best there was and each time I ride *[pause]* the circle gets smaller *[pause]*. But I'm feeling something now, something strange when I'm driving that circle... hot breath on the back of my neck, hotter and hotter each time and a voice with that fire saying in breaths that scorch my skin, saying, 'FLY' or... or maybe 'DIE', and sometimes I hear 'SPEED' and then it gets to sounding like 'BLEED' or 'FAST' that becomes 'LAST' that becomes 'GOLDEN—HORN—HOOLI-GAN... THIS IS THE LAST' *[he stands silent, head down in front of car for a few seconds, then slowly raises his head]* and... the circles... getting smaller... and smaller... and the breaths getting hotter... and hotter... until I feel as though the car is just spinning... spinning

✛ 61 ✛

from its centre… spinning on its axis, faster and faster and my skin glowing red and then smouldering and then bursting into flames until Golden-Horn-Hooligan and Pope-Panther are just one whirring ball of flames… like a top that has exploded into fire… *[He stops and resumes his original position on the bonnet of Pope-Panther. He puts his head in his hands for a few moments and then lifts his face so that the light falls upon it.]* Boooom!! Just like a top.

AMERICAN–SPEEDWAY–FEVER–TRASH

SCENE

Car soundtrack. Two men in red leather stand slight left of stage. One calmly adjusts his crash helmet while the other, anxious and sweating, grips his in his hands. They stand like this for… say… one nailbiting minute.

EX-VALENTINE: *[suddenly, anxiously]* I can't race, Chassey, I can't, I just can't race!!

CHASSEY: *[slowly]* Fuck you, ex-Valentine, you asshole-cunt, put your cunt-crash-helmet on.

EX-VALENTINE: Chassey! I'm afraid. I see wheels turning… flaming… on fire! I see chequered flags of blood! I'm afraid… Chassey… scared… I… I… I dreamed…

CHASSEY: *[slowly]* Fuck you, ex-Valentine, you asshole cunt, put your cunt-crash-helmet on. I mean it.

EX-VALENTINE: *[hysterical]* Chassey… I think I got American-Speedway-Feev…

> *[CHASSEY turns violent and punches EX-VALENTINE's face hard, hard to the ground—grabs him by the collar.]*

CHASSEY: *[violently]* No cunt-brother will ever say that to me again. Remember Junk? Greatest American Speedway driver. Now cunt-stinking-yellow-chicken-grease-monkey-working under hot-rods for 20 skins a day—not you—Ex-Valentine—you ain't got it—not like cunt-Junk—you ain't got it—you ain't got cunt-American-Speed-way-Fever-cunt. *[Lights]*

CURTAIN

GREASY–HOT–ROD–CREAM

SCENE

A garage. Tyres, a few engines, a few tools. The sound of revving vehicles. The body of a really big-big-red-greasy-car with lots of chrome and something like "HOT-STUFF" written in flames down the side. A stocking hangs from the ariel. The bomb rocks on its bricks. Inside a MAN and GIRL fuck. The radio on.

GIRL: Oh you big greasy fucker cock, give it to me give it to me fuck. Stick it I'm ready I'm I'm oh cunt stick it stick it give it to me give it to me you big fucking greasy cocker shit.

MAN: *[greasy]* You got it shit-tits. King king king ugh you want it got it want it little fucker-tits got it have it spear cunt fucka shit-doll yours yours yours, yo-o-ours ughh motor-cunt ugghh yours kiss me and ev'ry little bit you're hit.

GIRL: Bring me oh bring me grease-monkey fucker-ass stick s'more smear me monster-fuck wet sing it monster and bring me sing it and bring me in Jesus Joe's hot-rod.

MAN: *[greasy]* Take it girl kiss me girl take it girl kiss me girl in Jesus-Joe's-hot-rod-car.

The radio gets louder drowning them as the silver curtain closes.

CURTAIN

GREASE–GUN–SHOOTER

SCENE

Grease-gun-shooter sits, his two feet apart; he is white, only he is black from head to feet and skinny. He is thinking out loud and sometimes squirting grease into a bucket with his big-grease-gun-shooter and we soon feel sorry for him as he gets none of the glory that the big men who drive the red-flame devils get. He sits sad. Centre stage of him is a big racing car in bits with Fat Mama written on the side. You can sometimes hear cars off-stage.

GREASE—GUN—SHOOTER: *[sadly]* Life is an engine, an ass, an engine-ass, thankless to grease-gun, to shooter blood, to piss oil in buckets *[he squirts]* while big-white-teeth garbage in my cars chew gum win cunts in cars while shooter-greasy-shooter fucks smoke pipes. Line 'em up for the greasy–grease–gun–shooter: oil change shooter, *[still sadder]* punture shooter old boy puncture. Grease-gun got a blow-out while cheesey-white blows-off *[he squirts more]*. Greasy is a black, greasy is a white, greasy sleeps with bombs all night. *[He squirts, stands, oh! so sadly wipes his face with a rag, G.G.S. in black, then gestures]* Sample the cunt, Gunner, Demonbitch, Shark-fire, hot-hot-hot-hot. *[Quietly, sadly]*. Roll over Fat Mama, I'm comin' in.

CURTAIN

SALOMÉ

The Seven Veils
Dialogue with the Baptist
Salomé's Reward
The Chop
The Platter

Young girl enters and moves to centre/front of stage.

VESTAL VIRGIN: *[deadpan]* The story of Salomé and John the Baptist in five parts. See this mess of thorns.

THE SEVEN VEILS

Arabic wailing and bells. All props, crown, throne etc must look like they were made by children. KING HEROD sits on throne centre-left oggling a despondent SALOMÉ who sulks and sighs and allows her heavenly body to pursue conquettishly the serpentine rhythms of music in a manner of cruel titillation. Her slips, shrugs and sudden spasms are a cruel test for the ancient but riggish King. SALOMÉ is bored and finds small pleasure in the torment.

KING HEROD: What ails thee, my precious Salomé? What is it that has put your pretty little nose so out of joint? You need some cheer. Dance for me, my peach, your King is old and finds small joy in his waning years. Dance for your King and brighten an old man's corner with your youthful fulgence. Come, my petal, dance and you shall be rewarded.

SALOMÉ *[with a pout]* A reward?
If it be your wish, my King.
Music! Let's have some life!
Your Majesty, 'The Dance of the Seven Veils'.

The music pulses and snakes, but Salomé remains stock-still, facing Herod. She removes, one by one, the veils that are bound about her body. Her hair is as liquid gold. Her lips are blood-heavy and as clinquant as cut rubies. Her teeth are like pearls. Her breasts are hillocks of honeycoloured sand. Her quim is shielded by a fine lace.

KING HEROD: *[increasingly delirious]* One!… oh! see how it flutters from her hand. Two!… ohh! downward like a dying bird… THREE!… oh beautiful Salomé I love you… Oh! now, FOUR!… see how the veils cause the floor to storm, yet their absence reveals such still and silent flesh… FIVE!… oh my heart pounds out to you. What you create with your seven veils God, creaking at the hinges, could never approach with his seven days. Oh… SIX!!
[Herod clutches painfully at his heart as he collapses.]

Enter John the Baptist in camel skins.

JOHN THE BAPITIST: What evil here?

SALOMÉ: *[calling to the wings]* Seize him guards! Seize the Baptist!

BLACKOUT

VESTAL VIRGIN enters and introduces the play thus:

VESTAL VIRGIN: *[deadpan]* Play number two is entitled 'Dialogue with the Baptist'. *[Moves to far back corner and watches.]*

DIALOGUE WITH THE BAPTIST

A clumsy wooden kennel with a wire-screen frontage incarcerates JOHN THE BAPTIST like an animal. SALOMÉ sits atop the box swinging one long bright naked leg in front of the cage. One hand slips beneath her robe, while the other holds a large apple which she eats. Her toenails are painted the colour of blood. Salomé fingers herself.

JOHN THE BAPTIST: I, John the Baptist, even while caged like a dog, do not grovel so deep into the muck as you, Salomé. You are sin. Lucifer, the dark angel, watches over you knowing that one day he will claim you. You are the wicked and you have his mark upon you. Repent now or suffer horrors too vile to mention.

SALOMÉ: If I have my way, pompous turd, you won't have a brain for much longer! *[She laughs.]*

JOHN THE BAPTIST: I, John the Baptist, bound in affliction and iron, kept like a dog in a cage, will never know pain as you will one day know, Salomé. Spawn of incest, you are damned for eternity. Too vile for the grave, too vile for the grave. You are beyond redemption! Marked with devil blood, ruled by the moon! O hellish vixen! O cloven gender!

SALOMÉ: Cleanse me, Baptist. Take this yoke, the moon, under which ah slave, the terrible Emperess of mah body. Its climate, its seasons. I am woman. Cleanse me. Wash away all that's comely. Chasten me, Baptist, with your waters.

The moon appears above them. It is a gold platter.

JOHN THE BAPTIST: Get thee behind me, Satan! A single strand of your hair would pollute the sacred Jordan river. Was it you who dipped her toe in what is now called the DEAD SEA? I would suffer an eternity in darkness, clothed in worms, rather than make a mockery of the blessed mystery of baptism.

SALOMÉ: Suit yourself, dick breath!

The moon lowers itself, appears to hover just above and behind SALOMÉ's head.

See, Baptist. The moon sanctifies me. It sits behind my crown of curls like a gloriole.

BLACKOUT

VESTAL VIRGIN: Play number three is entitled 'Salomé's Reward'.

SALOMÉ'S REWARD

Single spot-light illuminates SALOMÉ centre-stage.

SALOMÉ: *[In an evil whisper]* My mouth asks for it. My heart weeps for it! My cunt yearns for it!! The moon, in turn, demands it. THE HEAD OF JOHN THE B.!!

BLACKOUT

VESTAL VIRGIN: The fourth play is entitled 'The Chop'. *[Stands back; fingers herself absent-mindedly as she looks on.]*

THE CHOP

As in the remarkable painting by Puvis de Chavannes the scene is thus: (left to right) NEGRO with axe; JOHN THE BAPTIST, hands roped and kneeling; SALOMÉ, hand working diligently between her sugar thighs.

.JOHN THE BAPTIST: All Heaven and Hell are watching, evil one! The angels puff up the clouds for me, the poker is in the furnace for you! *[He looks heavenward.]* I am ready, Lord!

SALOMÉ: *[in climactic ecstasy]*… And so am I! Let the axe drop, and silence this fucking do-gooder!

JOHN THE BAPTIST: I go to my God. Though narrow are the gates, he will show the way.

The moon blinks on and blood runs down the insides of SALOMÉ's dress.

BLACKOUT *as axe falls.*

VESTAL VIRGIN: The last play is entitled 'The Platter'.

THE PLATTER

> *KING HEROD, recovered from his coronary, on throne with large piece of chicken in hand. Enter NEGRO with head of JOHN THE BAPTIST, on a platter. The head must be infinitely bloody and so on. HEROD recoils in horror.*

KING HEROD: *[Clutching his problem heart]* Wha… what is that!?

NEGRO: This my most worthy master is the head of John the Baptist… minus the tongue, which Salomé demanded for herself. She said to inform you that you may eat the head but she's gunna teach her cunt to talk good.

> Pause

> *A pre-pubescent girl enters, naked but covered in bloody hand-prints.*

GIRL: *[Deadpan]* The end.

BLACKOUT

FROM HER TO ETERNITY

The Black Pearl

Cabin Fever!
Well of Misery
From Her to Eternity
Saint Huck
Wings off Flies
A Box for Black Paul

The Moon is in the Gutter
Just a Closer Walk With Thee
The Six Strings that Drew Blood
The Million Dollar Hands of Roberto Duran

Oh I Love You Much Too Much

H.M.S. Britain 1982

THE BLACK PEARL

Nocbi eternus in faece cloaca, in exsilium cum catarax optico. Corpus leperum, oh, corpus leperum, similis albino papyrus vexillum. Ego surrendus. Deus non capit captivum. Eus non capit captivum. Ego Exceptum.

We absorb the image, the glistening body-form, that *is* and will continue to be the *life*-source, the centrifugal axis to our attentions. We squint. We scrutinise but it is a dying, dying sun that lays a pale blanket over our point of conjecture, that turns the mud-pool into a Great Gilded Dish, flat 'n' round. We skirt the perimeter, lifting our eyes up from the central mystery only to reaffirm that We Are Still on Solid Ground. We are.

Ego est protag. Doggéd.

Steam rises from the figure in coils. The figure has not moved for one entire circumnavigation. View-point follows view-point in an attractive circular sequence. We fear our eyes will betray us, like so many times before, so we imbibe the information with greater urgency. The golden sun is sinking. Our minds race and never rest. We absorb, we digest, we interpret, we construct. Our heads pound with sickly poetry. The mist is trapped beneath the tree-tops. It hangs in veils. It hangs in veils. Trees and bushes become so many jilted brides.

The dark out-land will smell of *death* before the next sun-rise. How do we know this? We know, now, that it was *death* that robbed the weeping brides for from behind their veils fall heavy tears that splash into the gilded dish. A morsel lies, uneaten in the centre of the dish. You can find a potential husband anywhere but good food will soon go rotten. By all indications the reception was a sumptuous affair. We identify the wasted morsel as a crustacean, possibly a prawn. Our eyes strain for further evidence. Steam rises from it in coils.

We see that his knees are drawn up to his chest and that he lies naked upon his side, forgotten. We see that the pale orange glow filtering through the mist catches the beads of moisture upon his body. From the perimeter his skin appears segmented like the exo-skeleton of a cray or prawn. He lies naked upon his side. One pitch-black pearl stares up, frozen. We suppose it to be a death-stare until, without so much as one tendon flinching, in face or body, it pleaded, this pitch-black pearl, pleaded for death, and we stare aghast. Our hearts swell in sympathy. Our eyes well in misery and tears flow freely down our cheeks. They mingle with those of the jilted brides who have not stopped, not even for a moment. We stretch out our arms to him, but in vain for, though we are tall men, we cannot reach him. Still he does not move, nor his eye. We try to call him, but we have not been given voices yet. Secure in the knowledge that we are many and possessed by the urge to lend assistance we step bravely across the perimeter. But noble intentions, nay, nor brave steps sate the glutinous malacostoma. Lo! the black mud sucks all feet bare of boots and we are forced to lurch back lest we are fully devoured. We quiver in the dark, the sun gone now and with it its golden glow.

O gone is the sun. At home our pining Nancys lie warmly waiting. O gone is the glow. Our boots are full of black mud. We scrape and scrape but they are ruined. How can we attend the reception with one soggy boot? We cannot! Alas, we must let gold tarnish and the good food rot!

The forgotten crustacean decays rapidly, turning a smokey grey. The rot works like a cancer from the under-side upon the black-green dish. Within minutes almost half the morsel has been eaten away. It is disappearing before our eyes. Only one pitch-black pearl stares up, pleading. A swarm of insects attack what remains of his diminishing frame, sucking and stinging him, causing his skin to blossom with welts and bites. We are impotent to help and we hang our heads in respect for his suffering. Again our emotions shame us for we cannot suppress one final bitter tear. It emerges the shape and weight of an oval locket that springs open to reveal the image of a little girl. She has a face of unearthly countenance, like a child-saint. We recognise her as if she is one of our own but for the moment cannot place her. The locket falls and is consumed. We make to retrieve it as one clutches at the phantom of a loved one. Gone. In its place our own reflected image becomes clearer as the mud settles. We recoil in horror. Our faces are frozen there for a moment upon the surface. Screwed and pumped with blood they are, our eyes bugged and full of hatred. Our mouths are twisted into grimaces of rage. Split purple lips form obscenities midst the yellow froth. Spittle runs freely and our hair is caked in dirt and the shit of animals. In our fists, knuckles showing white, are all manner of makeshift weapons, shears, picks, homemade clubs, lengths of rope, kitchen knives and corn-scythes that we wave pel-mel above our heads.

Night removes its cloak and the pit turns blacker than *death*. Beasts howl like hags at a wake. We do not hear them. We grope for small bushes. We uproot them. We soak their tops in gasoline and ignite them. We hold them at arm's length toward the centre, making a circle of fire. Black smoke rises up and is trapped beneath the tree-tops. The smoke hangs in veils. The trees become so many grieving mothers. Their faces are set as stone, beyond tears. That which robbed them of a wedding, that which snatched their only child, *must* take one last man this night. But who? The wheel of night diminishes as the firelight moves across the surface toward the centre. Only his head remains, and his eye, no longer pleading, no. That black coal *mocks* us all now. We recall the child-saint. We push our fingers through the holes in the little red dress we find fouled and bloody in our hands. We roar at this monstrous trickery in silence. The grieving mothers twist and shudder and tear their mourning veils from their faces. And as all rage and vengeance at last takes focus, we know we must work fast. His life is ours. It is a point of honour. We cannot be deprived. In a matter of seconds he will be gone. Death will not cheat us again. We must work fast. We must work fast and hard, that pitch-black pearl.

SUNDAYS SLAVE

Sunday's got a slave
Monday's got one too
From a manger of hay
To a stoney cold tomb
This master I serve
has a woman's name
I play a woman's game
Bound in affliction + iron
in affliction + iron to remain
Sunday's slave

Trailblazing 6th

16

but you've been this road, like a has a whore

this "road of rocks" of which you speak, you've never walked that road before
If I got a "heart of stone", then your feet sure must be sore
We'll you talk of the house of love "as if it never had a door
No Baby I don't love you anymore But that ain't stopped you before that's how come are

There's no sense in standing in the hall
And I don't talk of a road of rocks, this heart can't hear that anymore
Don't speak of a heart of stone, stop this your speaking, you've
show me 'the house of love', is it it never had a door as if you've walked that never road before
You speak about f this
Booy I dont love you, anymore

My shadow of my — — have just faded into yours
The debris of our undoing is strewn across the floor
All these tears your shedding well you should've thought of that before
M • L PIXOTE •

CABIN FEVER!

The Captain's fore-arm like buncht-up rope,
With A-N-I-T-A wrigglin free outa skull 'n' dagger
And a portrait of Christ, nailed to an anchor,
Etched into the upper…
Slams his fucken tin dish down.
Our Captain takes time to crush
Some bloo-bottles glowin in his gruel,
With a lump in his throat and lumpy mush,
Thumbing a scrap-book stuck up with clag
And a morbid lump of love in his flag.
Done is the kissing, now all that remains
Is to sail forever upon the stain.
Cabin Fever!O, O O Cabin Fever!
The Captain's free hand is a cleaver
With which he fashions his beard and rations his jerky,
And carves his peg outa the finest mahogany!
Or was it ebony? Yeah, it was ebony!
He tallys up his loneliness notch by notch,
For the sea offers nuthin to hold or touch.
Notch by notch, winter by winter,
Notch by notch, winter by winter.
Now his leg is whittled right down to a splinter.
O, O Cabin Fever! Cabin Fever!
O the rollin sea still rollin on!
She's everywhere! now that she's gone! Gone! Gone!
O Cabin Fever! O Cabin Fever!

Welcome to the table, his belovéd-unconscious
Raisin her nest of hair from her crooks
And strugglin to summon up one of her looks!
His arm now, like coiled s-s-s-snakes,
Whips all the bottles that he's drunked
Like crystal skittles about the cabin
Of a ship they'd been sailing five years sunken.

WELL OF MISERY

Along crags and sunless cracks I go
Up rib of rock, down spine of stone
I dare not slumber where the night winds whistle
Lest her creeping soul clutch this heart of thistle.

O the same God that abandoned her
Has in turn abandoned me
And softening the turf with my tears
I dug a well of misery.

And in that well of misery
Hangs a bucket full of sorrow
Which swings slow and aching like a bell
Its toll is dead and hollow.

Down that well lies the long-lost dress
Of my little floating girl
That muffles a tear that you let fall
All down the well of misery.

Put your shoulder to the handle if you dare
And hoist that bucket hither
Crank and hoist and hoist and crank
'Til your muscles waste and wither.

O the same God that abandoned her
Has in turn abandoned me
Deep in the Desert of Despair
I wait at the Well of Misery.

FROM HER TO ETERNITY

Ah wanna tell ya bout a girl
You know, she lives in Room 29
Why that's the one right up top a mine
Ah start to cry, ah start to cry-y
O ah hear her walkin
Walkin barefoot cross the floor-boards
All through this lonesome night
And ah hear her crying too
Hot tears come splashin down
Leakin through the cracks
Down upon my face, ah catch em in my mouth!
Walk 'n' Cry, Walk 'n' Cry-y!!
From her to eternity
From her to eternity
From her to eternity
Ah read her diary on her sheets
Scrutinizin evry lil piece of dirt.
Tore out a page 'n' stufft if inside my shirt.
Fled outa the window
And shinning it down the vine
Outa her nightmare and back into mine.
Mine! O mine!
From her to eternity
From her to eternity
From her to eternity
Cry! Cry! Cry!
She's wearin them bloo-stockens, ah bet!
And standin like this with my ear to the ceiling
Listen ah know it must sound absurd
But ah can hear the most melancholy sound
Ah ever heard!
Walk 'n' Cry! Kneel 'n' Cry-y!
From her to eternity
From her to eternity.

O tell me why? why? why?
Why the ceiling still shakes?
Why the furniture turns to serpents 'n' snakes?

This desire to possess her is a wound
And it's naggin at me like a shrew
But ah know that to possess her
Is therefore not to desire her
O, O O then ya know, that lil girl would just have to go!
Go! Go-o-o! From her to eternity

CROOKED RIVER

'O sullen river, wide + weary, what are you running too?"
"To a watery grave, O my doomed sailor, to the grave I'm taking you "
"O swollen river, banks a bursting, sound the horn amongst the crew
" Pray not for them 'o foolish sailor, for they do not pray for you

"O fugitive river, sleepless water, what are you running
                                                    from?"
o' this caching burden, O restless

SAINT HUCK

Born of the river,
Born of its never-changing, ever-changing murky water.
Old river-boat keeps rolling along
Through the great grey greasy city,
Huck standing like a saint upon its deck.
If ya wanna catch a saint,
Then bait ya hook. Let's take a walk…

'O come to me! O come to me!' is what the dirty city
Say to Huck.
He go woah-woah, woah woah!
Saint Huck! Huck!

Straight into the arms of the city go Huck,
Down the beckonin streets of opportunity.
Huck whistles his favourite river-song…
And a bad-bline-nigger at the piano
Puts a sinister-bloo-lilt to that sing-a-long.
Huck senses something's wrong!
Sirens wail in the city,
And lil-Ulysses turn to putty.
Ol man River's got a bone to pick!
Our boy's hardly got a bone to suck!
He goa woah-whoa, woah woah!
Saint Huck! Huck!

The moon, its huge cycloptic eye
Watches the city streets contract,
Watchem twist and cripple and crack.
Saint Huck goes on a dog's leg now
Saint Huck goes on a dog's leg now.

Why, you know the story!
Ya wake up one morning and ya find you're a thug
Cracking ya knuckles in some dive,
Ya fingers hot and itchin, blowin smoke rings,
Ya bull-neck bristlin…
Still Huck he ventures on whistlin.

And Death reckons Huckleberry's time is up.
O woah woah woah woah!
Saint Huck! Huck!

Yonder go Huck, minus pocket-watch an' wallet gone,
Skin shrink-wraps his skeleton.
No wonder he git thinner, wot with his cold 'n' skinny dinners!
Saint Huck-a-Saint Elvis, Saint Huck-a-Saint Elvis
O you remember the song ya used to sing-a-long
Shifting the river-trade on that ol steamer
Life is just a dream!
But ya traded in the mighty ol man River
For the dirty ol man Latrine!
The brothel shift
The hustle 'n' the bustle and the green-back's rustle
And all the sexy cash
And the randy cars
And the two dollar fucks
O, O O ya outa luck, outa luck
Woah-woah-woah-woah
Saint Huck! Huck!

These are the tracks of deception.
They lead to the heart of despair.
Huck whistles like he just don't care
That in the pocket of the jacket is a chamber,
And a lead pellet sleeps in there.
Wake up!
Huck whistles and he kneels and he lays down there.

See ya Huck. Good luck!
A smoke ring hovers above his head.
And the rats and the dogs and the men all come
And put a bullet through his eye.
And the drip and the drip and the drip of the Mississippi crying,
And Saint Huck has his own Mississippi just rolling by him.
He goes, he goes woah-woah-woah, woah-woah-woah!
Saint Huck! Saint Huck!
Saint Huck! Saint Huck!

So, there's a space on the wall
Where the shotgun hang
Ma, that don't necessarily mean a thing
And those marks on the floor
Where this so-called deed was done
They could be anything
Are ya gunna sit at the window
+ weep all night?
Over something that might never been.

Pistol is going crazy in mah hands
The wheels are turning round + round + round
And nothing that stood continues to
stand
Even the sun is shrinking behind a cover of.

ME + THE WHEELS ARE THE
ONLY SOUND

(i)
Sun is low + pinking there   when the sun goes down
Funnel of dust, a big red sail + my work is done
Sun is slowly sinking there
Tunnel of dust, a big red sail
Snakes bake on the hot rocks where   I can do anything
I grab them suckers by the tail,   She is my sceptre my golden
(ii)
My hands are two lunatic kings t down the road, another for
While I've been sleeping I've watched them work
My hands are two jealous kings
While I sleep I've watched them working
All the dead I've left behind us
Are little gifts I've shot for her
(iii)
Ma, ya know I see you've seen the space upon
Where the shotgun used t- hang
Ma, I see you've seen the space
Where the shotgun used to hang
those marks on the floor
they could be anything

WINGS OFF FLIES

She loves me, she loves me not
She loves me, she loves me not.

Well I've spent seven days and seven nights
Trying to get sunk in this brine
Don't turn on your water-works
'Cause I've got me a pair of water-wings, right?!
Insects suicide against the window
And my heart goes out to those little flies
There's a buzzing in my ear
But it's more of her blackmail, ham Shakespeare and lies.
Wings off flies
She loves me, she loves me not
O, O O O oh she loves me not!

Lord, I've discovered the recipe of Heaven
You get solitude and mix with sanctuary and silence
Then bake it!
Listen, I plead guilty to misanthropy
So hang me! And appreciate it!
Witness her gate-crash my tiny hell
With some obscene tête-à-tête
If you want to talk to me about love and pain
Consult my ulcer, it'd be happy to co-operate.
Wings off flies
She loves me, she loves me not
Hey Joe, another ought to do the job.

Time to drown our little fire, you can keep the ashes
Now bye bye, bye bye, see you in a pig's eye!
I will be one, in need of no-one
In this, my deepest dire…
Fill her up, Joe…
Hey! I am obliged! I AM OBLIGED!
Wings off flies
She loves me, she loves me not.

A BOX FOR BLACK PAUL

Who'll build a box for Black Paul?
I'm enquiring on behalf of his soul.
I'd be beholden to you all
For a little information, just some kind of indication
Just who will dig the hole.

When you've done ransacking his room,
Grabbing anything that shines,
Throw the scraps down on the street,
Like all his books and his notes,
All his books and his notes and all the junk that he wrote,
The whole fucking lot right up in smoke.
Ain't there nothing sacred anymore?
Who will build a box for Black Paul?

And they're shooting off his guns,
And they're shooting off their mouths,
Saying 'Fuck with us ... and die!'
(But see that rat of fear go scuttle in their skulls)
'Cover that eye!' 'Cover that frozen eye!'
Black puppet, in a heap up against the stoning-wall,
Blood puppet go to sleep, Mama won't scold you anymore.
Armies of ants wade up the little red streams
Heading for the mother-pool.
O Lord it's cruel! O man it's hot!
And some of those ants they just clot to the spot.
Who cast the first stone at Black Paul?

'Don't ask us', say the critics and the hacks
The pen-pushers and the quacks
'We jes cum to git dah facks!!'
'We jes cum to git dah facks!!'

Here is the hammer that built the scaffold
And built the box,
Here is the shovel that dug the hole
In this ground of rocks,
And here is the pile of stones!

And for each one planted, God only knows,
A blood-rose grown...

These are the *true* Demon-Flowers!
These are the *true* Demon-Flowers!
Stand back everyone! Blood-black every one!

Who'll build a box for Black Paul?
Who'll carry it up the hill?

'Not I', said the widow, adjusting her veil
'Ah will not drive the nail,
Or cart his puppet-body home
For ah done that one thousand times before
Yeah! ah done that one thousand times or more,
And why should ah dress his wounds
When he has wounded my dress, nightly,
Right across the floor?'

Who'll build a box for Black Paul?
And who'll carry it up the hill?
Who'll bury him in the black soil?

From the woods and the thickets
Come the ghosts of his victims
'We love you!'
'*I* love you!'
And 'This won't hurt a bit,
We'll go up, up, up, up, up into Death
Up, up, up, up. Inhale its breath!
Oh O, Death favours those that favour Death'.

Here is the stone, and this is the inscription that it bears:
'Below Lies Black Paul, Under The Upper
But Above And Beyond The Surface-Flat-Fall There'.

And all the angels come on down
And all the men and women crowd around
And all the widows weeping into their skirts
And all the little girls and the little boys

And all the scribes with pens poised
And all the hullaballoo, and all the noise
All the hallaballoo, all the noise
All the hallaballoo and all of the noise.

Black Paul clears his throat of black blood
And sings in the voice of a lonely boy ...

    Well I have cried one thousand tears
    I've cried a thousand tears, it's true
    And the next stormy night you know
    That I'm still crying them for you.

    Well I had a girl she was so sweet,
    Red dress, and long red hair hanging down,
    And heaven just ain't heaven
    Without that little girl hanging around.

    Well you know I've been a bad man
    And Lord knows I've done some good things too
    But I confess, my soul will never rest
    Until you, until you build,
    Until you build a box for my girl too.

THE MOON IS IN THE GUTTER

The moon is in the.gutter
And the stars wash down the sink
I am the king of the blues
I scrape the clay off my shoes
And wade down the gutter and the moon.

The moon blinds my eye with opal cataracts
As I cut through the saw-mills and the stacks,
Leaping over the gully where I would one day take Lucy
Then wash up my hands in the gully and the moon.

Such a long way from home, just me and
The moon is in the gutter
All my plans are flushed down the drain
I wonder lonely as a cloud
Over memories at her mound
Then lie down in the bitter gutter moon.

JUST A CLOSER WALK WITH THEE

Just a closer walk with thee
Come back, honey, to me
Then I'll be moving up close to thee
O let it be, O Lord, let it be.

I go to the garden all alone
Deception lurking at every turn
If to have that rose I must hold the thorn
Then let it be, O Lord, let it be.

Love's sweet garden overgrown
Gone is the rose and deep is the thorn
If I must walk these paths alone
Then let it be, please Lord, on up to thee.

THE SIX STRINGS THAT DREW BLOOD

Guitar thug blew into town
His eyes like wheels spinnin' round
And jerkin' off at every sound
Layin' all his crosses down
He got six strings
The six strings that drew blood
He got six strings
Six strings that drew blood.

The bar is full of holy Joes
Holy holy ho-leerio
Round the neck of our consumptive rose
Is the root of all his sorrow
He got six strings
Six strings that drew blood.

Holy holy ho-leerio
Holy holy ho-leerio
Holy holy ho-leerio
Six strings that drew blood.

In the bathroom under cover
He turns on one tap to discover
That he's smashed his teeth out on the other
And he says to the mirror 'Hey don't fuck me brother
cause I've got six strings'
Yeah six strings that drew blood.

With the runt of reputation they call rat fame
Top E as a tourniquet
A low tune whistles across his grave
Forever the master and the slave
Of his six strings.

Holy holy ho-leerio
Holy holy ho-leerio
Holy holy ho-leerio
Six strings that drew blood.

THE MILLION DOLLAR HANDS
OF ROBERTO DURAN

My slumming fingers kick around
A pie-jaw locked into fist
Wrapped in little pillows fulla brick
I'm searching for a brick-woman
Jelly-babies stick to the roof of my mouth
Sucked-up and regretting ever reaching out
Through the ropes
Mitts off! My kingly man-handle
That I wash up in the pan of some 200 lb. shit-can
Keep my corner spick n spick n span
I'm searching for a brick-woman
Cause I'm a brick-man
Sugar-baby sucked up and spat out on the mat
O sometime I want you to sit me down
And make me understand, how did
These gloves in the trash-can get
I'm gunna keeell your muther
You're a dead man
The one million dollar hands
of Roberto Duran.

O I LOVE YOU MUCH TOO MUCH

Oh I love you much too much
Slow-talking pain
comes on like a rolling grub,
Smothers like a snail's foot
Would a tiny lady bug,
Robs my yellow garden bright
Of it's spring-time sunshine breath
Hairy stalk, pod, bud, seed, bead
Loving bee, gnome, elf, self: Death.

WHEN THE SUN GOES DOWN   by N.CAVE 30/10/1984
(and my work is done)

Memory is the boss-driver
And he wears razors on his spurs
Kicks my ribs to ribbons   *Oh Sick Friday*
Flogs me open like a girl
Memory rides and rides
This nightly black-gallop-tragic
And sleep is my wide-eyed quarry
~~Stassed by reigns of Steinway wire~~ *a restless, nervous*
                                                    maverick
Chaffing on the ~~fucken~~ bit
On ~~the whole fucken lot of it~~ *bleed* + *On the whole lot of it*
My ~~agony-~~jaws a~~booth as~~ *bleed +* foam and ~~red~~ froth
And gums livid with steely spit
Night after night, this black-gallop-tragic
Through field upon field of thistle and briar
Tall as a boy. ~~Liar! Liar!~~
Raking my ~~underside~~ *bloody underside*
Wide as the world, *wide as the world*
A trail of blood-splash ad Memory rides
O Memory is the boss-rider's tool
With spinning razors on his spurs
And as the sun goes down and my work is done
He comes and I freeze *+ freeze*
For he rides most at night and hard   *heels*
With silver spinning razors on his skinning ~~spurs~~
Rides the black-gallop-tragic
He comes, down the stable halls
The soung of his steps pretty like little bells
Like little stepping girls
Like clusters of ~~Silver~~ singing bellss
And it is like a cold long knife
And cold I say *wo boy wo*
~~Wo boy wo~~ *But memory rides me every night*
But sleep is a suckling
On a road *, + I say wo boy wo*
But sleep is a baby blind on the road
                --the end--

GM D# GM D#   B6 AM GM D#G
D#G D9 A G D#G D#G

H.M.S. BRITAIN 1982

19 YEARS moribund, suffering the congenital cancer of childhood, c/w adolescence its fearful retrograde. Mother crossed herself as P. Rock bumped me off the sick list. 1982 and 6 years hence. I must say, from the outset, that really I am not qualified to comment. I mean, the B.P. weren't there. That is, we'd mutinied early on (HMS Britain was a good ship we just got sick of doing all the rowing, keeping the old tub afloat so to speak). Even still, from either side of the moat that one spent this miserable year it can only be argued that this was yet another of musical mediocrity plop, plop, plop, a dying country spinning slowly on its axis in its own sludge aided in its demise by MOVEMENTS and COLLECTIVES promoted by 'the perverts, perverters of language' (Ezra Pound), the press-gang such as the nauseating collective incorp. SG Children-M Violets—SD Cult-D Society and So On—which I was asked to write about, presumably because the BP have now been given the honorary title of forefathers to the 'New-Super-death Tribe' by the above mentioned PG, thankyou but no thankyou and again I thank no. Papers'-Tigers, all, serving only to disguise the main issues and so on, a 'great' band having for their own part an obligation to exploit their most hidden desires and so on which by definition alienates them, given that all true desire is self-obsessive and individualist and so on and also that a 'GREAT' song must have the inna'te ability to touch the private soul of the listener invoking private response and with that in mind a 'GREAT' song is therefore multi-dimensional, if you get my drift and that SG Children-SD Cult and so on REFLECT if anything (REFLECT being the big word here) 'The Mood of the Times' if I may use this sickening expression, ie a desire for a bit more violence and so on and that kind of stuff and so on and in my most sought after opinion a group that REFLECTS anything other than their own isiosyncratic vision is not worth a pinch and anyway that is enough of that full stop. In conclusion, the Birth.P. are in essence a *slug*, nomadic, and their journey is slow and painful and always forward and their trail of slime is their art and so on and they are barely conscious of its issue which bears little resemblance to anything bar ourselves and we make no excuses for that.

BLINE LEMON JEFFERSON

BLINE LEMON JEFFERSON

I

Bline Lemon Jefferson is a-comin. Tap tap tapping with his cane. Bline
Lemon Jefferson is a-comin. Tap a tap a tappin with his cane. O see that
yonder field all gone to seed? Well see the corner where the kudzu kills
the sycamore and two oily black crows like Madonnas teeter there upon?
It is against that laden trunk, the weary negro will pull his Dobro round
and with his other hand grope and find a naked root risin from the eaten
soil, risin from a network of younger lesser roots like a swollen vein and
there upon that root he will perch, like a bigger blacker third bird.

II

Low an limply strummin forth, a gagging melody that strains for a
moment an is gone, from tin-pot geetar, airborn like the prodigal son an
what colour murder then? A moaning threnody unsung in veils of purple,
plum an bruise and floods of claret, cochineal an pewce. One last dark cry
from the noose's mouth an his stranglin-hand fell from its neck and took
up hiding in the left-side pocket of his trousers and so too, in turn, his
black-fist that mauled its hollow body ceased also, and to his other pocket
fled and it was there that they holed-up, those killingten, hidden from the
noon-day sun that bore down upon the knitted fields.

III

Behold the eyes of Bline Lemon Jefferson! Behold the eye-flesh and the
curdled inner-eye therein. O ah say, draw to, n look on; fear not, for he
will not return your stare. See! They have put nickels in his eyes! See!
Eclipsed they are by two silver-bloo lids, nickel-sized. Like the bells of
pearly shells, bloo-white and milk-pink film trammel an entire muted
spectrum upon its smitten surface. Behold the opal-cataracts that robbed
him of his sight and went an made him go bline.

IV

Stand toward and look across. This could well be God's own acre but
Lord knows, it is fucken well not. Let's go bang our broom-sticks on the
ceiling of the world. Let's goad out our sulking God who has bin doggo in

his poke since before ah can remember, since before his lil acre went to seed beneath a quilt of quitch and kudzu, cooch and crab and crawling dog-weed. O God of truth and troth, tend to your flock for they have strayed. We are creatures of grief and faith and we are bleeting at your gates. Give us shade. Give us shade. Give us shade.

V

Marvel, now, at the way the stoop of the old man's body is echoed in the sycamore as it too leans toward the earth. Bline Lemon Jefferson suffers a world that's void of light, but o it spills with sound. He hears the shrinking corset of kudzu bruise the mighty mainstem of the sycamore. He listens and he hears the tree's ancient limbs groan as it surrenders unto the killin woven vine. He hears its roots risin slowly from the sod as the tree is pulled over and down. He listens, now, to the sound of his own body in bondage, his spine and costal crumbling, his limbs enchained and his very lungs achin for air, collared and grounded and smitted by the stinging hail of life's smites. O, and now this creature of grief, bline and living in blooded blackness, must relive again and again, in retrospeck, all the tribulations of his past; and that of all, by God, is the hardest knock. It is now, beneath the sycamore, in the arms of its tortured shadow that Bline Lemon Jefferson recalls a time when his boots were black and the fields were yellah and even in the pitch of night there was a star to see or a slice of moon or a wick in a lamp to tender.

VI

Here cums the great Boss-driver
Krak krak krakken with his whip
O beware the crool Boss-driver
Krak krak krakken with his whip
Smith + Wessen cockt in his saddle-bag
So black-hands start pitchin hay real quick.

Ah wassa just 14 when ah lef home
The year wassa nineteen-tweeny-eight
Ah crosst the river into Clarkesdale
Workd in the fields from Can to Caint
Can hardly see when we're called in
Caint see a thing when we're sent out.

Early one mornin ah git the news
Say Hey Captn ah believe mah poor Ma-ma's dead
Pitchin hay early one mornin ah git the news
Say Hey, Boss mah poor Ma-ma's dead
Boss says he says Hey nigger if you don't
git back to work pronto you'll soon be dead too.

The devil's got your badge Boss
an white kill-hand dives into his saddle-purse.
Ah spin toward him like ah am summoned
O "there is a sin unto death" ah sayeth
and for a seck ah think this:
Ah'll be 15 cum tomorra morn;
and ah hit him with the hay-rake
in the crocker-bone.

VII

Ah calculate it being near on one quarter mile to the Arkansaw State Line
and that the river… bank to bank… is almost that distance again. Ah prize
the mighty Smith + Wessen free. Ah grab mah ol geetar… from yonder
tree… and ah leg it down the levee… in no time flat. Quickern you can
say… "Hay-rake hangin inna Boss-man's back"… Say ah… "O Lawd have
mercy on mah poor sinkin soul"… Well ah pushd off an mooved on in…
And ah walkd the blessed waves… And ah walkd as far as ah could… An
never bin able to swim… Ah guess ah musta walkd twenny-five minutes
under that water.
　　Ah cum out in Tennessee.
　　By the tenth mile ah was completely bline. Mah vagrant sight floats
somewhere… below the surface, for it is lost… and mine eyes… white as a
shroud and out of sight are washed from their sockets by that muddy
Mississippi ablution… and let us not forget… the burden of blood… borne
away… by that rolling river… and with it and away my iniquity gone
hateful, my sin… my sinner-mitts skinned… and lo my boss-blood n eye-
balls… all up the creek n down… my ablepsy being by my ablution… an
again pray let us not forget that fitted neatly in my sockets… where my eyes
once shone… were my bran new cataracts small n white n round like the
body of Christ… O Eucharist!… O Sacrament!… wafer thin and holy.
　　There issa mullet in the mud… on the floor of the Mississippi, that is
fixed upon somethin there… lurkin in the murk… O Lord… two river-
opals shot with blood… that roll n wink n roll n wink n roll n wink… O
Lord…

VIII

Then ah walked down the levee, ah guess about sixty miles in all. Ma-a-an, there was near onna thousan men cum lookin for me. Lemmee tell ya something, it weren't jes the Clarkesdale plantation that turned out for the hunt, no way. There hadn't bin a lynching in these parts since they caught Willy Christian milking the Salde boys' still near on two years ago. Boss Grobey, the Schultz brothers. Vernon Callihan. They all gave over their hounds and their hands. They brought down a black-tracker from Fern Valley and by noon-time the hunt was in full swing, up to the levee and way, way along. Listen, let it be known that all the blud-dogs and pro-trackers and pick-ups fulla dusty men and dusty boys gittin shit-faced on some cheap shit and wavin shot-guns around like toys and gazzaleen tins crashin around in back, ah mean, shit, enough gas to burn down a stable fulla niggers and rope, lawd, enough rope to loop and hog-tie the man-in-the-moon, and ah swear, it don't occur to no-one that maybe ah went and got across that river a-live. Come dusk, there was no question save which levee my lil fucken black body would cum wash up on. It mattered not, needless to say, the blud-hounds h-o-owled, denied and the black-tracks cursed, defeated and the mob turned their blud-shot eyes… back… to . . the fields… cheated.

IX

Cum that fat ol mornin sun
Long were the shadows of the trees.
Twas there upon that very limb
From which ah hung mah geetar
On that murderess morn—
Swinging long heavy arcs was hung
Another smokin charcoal man.

His name was Juke Boy Bonner… at least that's wot ahm led to unnerstand. Ah heard all this about the hound-dogs and the trackers and the lynchup some years on when ah came back to around these parts after being a famous bline star in Chicago… helluva town… helluva town.

X

O his road is dark and lonely
He don't drive no cadillac
O his road is dark and holy

He don't drive no cadillac
If that sky serves as his eye
Then the moon's a cataract

XI

Here, Chicago done and gone, and well inside the Memphis City Limits, perchd onna pickle-barrel, toonin down mah beloved home-made dobro, plantation-made that geetar, a long long time ago, ah be sittin a long long time ago.

Nine pilfered strings from the boss's sisters' pe-yana, stretchd across a lump o pine and treated with a coat of skunk-oil (or was it co-o-oon?). Would be a lie if ah said of it, that ah was given permission thus to use. In fact, if the truth be known, each night, a lil past curfew, in the ol corregated shed, on the steps, at the shelf, ah'd strain to reach the oil (if the truth be known) and then ah'd pour out a measure into a stolen servin spoon.

Sittin in the dark of the slavery-stable with a rag, that'd be a sin to say was mine, ah would dip into the heavy black lacker, then rub it deep into the thirsty pine.

XII

Now here, Memphis passd and well behind and the blooded sun ate at mah nape and the year was 1929. Ah had, upon this day, the occasion to feel like a winged angel, black n bline, sittin on a crate in the backblocks of Elysium, pickin tick n bird-louse from mah flap-sad pinions and pluckin, for thee, a lull-a-bye on the backbone offa fish-head.

Halleluja! Halleluja! Ahm fucken broke in Buffalo Springs! Yet it was here, at the Sunday afternoon meet of the General Association of the Buffalo Springs Baptist Corner, that the sound of a gee-tar, played fast as lightnin, rose above the racket n stink of mah darkness and caught mah ear. He said, "Mah name is Hopkins, Sam". Said, "Mah daddy fled the Clarkesdale plantation. He wassa urglee man"

Ah put him on toppa the truck where ah wassa sittin, yeah! And we had ourselves an a-so-see-ashon!! Ho! And he played uppa toppa that there truck, yep, an ah played some too, yep, and then after Sunnyland Slim an Bline Snooks Eaglin an Lightnin Hopkins, why, we all took off, leaving behind bleeding~angels to keep our seats warm.

Well now... we all took off from Buffalo Springs together.

XIII

Snooks Eaglin went bline in a brain tumour. His was not a religious experience as was the takin of mine eyes.

XIV

We travelled back up to Chicago.

THE FIRST-BORN IS DEAD

Tupelo
Say Goodbye to the Little Girl Tree
Train Long-Suffering
Black Crow King
Knockin' on Joe
Wanted Man
Blind Lemon Jefferson

TUPELO

Looka yonder!
Looka yonder!
Looka yonder!
A big black cloud come!
O comes to Tupelo. Comes to Tupelo.

Yonder on the horizon
Stopped at the mighty river and
Sucked the damn thing dry
Tupelo-o-o, O Tupelo.
In a valley hides a town called Tupelo.

Distant thunder rumble
Rumble hungry like the Beast
The Beast it cometh, cometh down
Wo wo wo-o-o, Tupelo bound
Tupelo-o-o, yeah Tupelo
The Beast it cometh, Tupelo bound.

Why the hen won't lay no egg
Cain't get that crock to crow
The nag is spooked and crazy
O God help Tupelo, O God help Tupelo!

Ya can say these streets are rivers
Ya can call these rivers streets
Ya can tell yaself ya dreaming buddy
But no sleep runs this deep.
Women at their windows,
Rain crashing on the pane
Writing in the frost Tupelo's shame
Tupelo's shame
O God help Tupelo! O God help Tupelo!

O go to sleep lil children,
The sandman's on his way
O go to sleep lil children,
The sandman's on his way.
But the lil children know,
They listen to the beating of their blood

They listen to the beating of their blood
The sandman's mud!
The sandman's mud!
And the black rain come down.
Water water everywhere
Where no bird can fly no fish can swim
No fish can swim
Until the King is born!
Until the King is born!
In Tupelo! Tupelo-o-o!
Til the King is born in Tupelo!

In a clap-board shack with a roof of tin
Where the rain came down and leaked within
A young mother frozen on a concrete floor
With a bottle and a box and a cradle of straw
Tupelo-o-o! O Tupelo!
With a bundle and a box and a cradle of straw.

Well Saturday gives what Sunday steals
And a child is born on his brother's heels
Come Sunday morn the first-born's dead
In a shoe-box tied with a ribbon of red
Tupelo-o-o! Hey Tupelo!
In a shoe-box tied with a ribbon of red.

O mama rock your lil one slow,
O ma-ma rock your baby.
O ma-ma rock your lil one slow
O God help Tupelo! O God help Tupelo!
Mama rock your lil one slow
The lil one will walk on Tupelo
Tupelo-o-o! Yeah Tupelo!
And carry the burden of Tupelo
Tupelo-o-o! O Tupelo!
Yeah! The King will walk on Tupelo
Tupelo-o-o! O Tupelo!
He carried the burden outa Tupelo!
Tupelo-o-o! Hey Tupelo!
You will reap just what you sow.

SAY GOODBYE TO THE LITTLE GIRL TREE

O say goodbye to the little girl tree
O you know that I must say goodbye
To the little girl tree.
This wall I built around you
Is made out of stone lies.
O little girl the truth would be
An axe in thee.
O father look to your daughter
Brick of grief and stricken mortar.
With this ring, this silver hoop of wire
I bind your maiden mainstem
Just to keep you as a child.

O say goodbye to the little girl tree
O you know that I must say goodbye
To my little girl tree.
How fast your candy bones
Reached out for me.
I must say goodbye to your brittle bones
Crying out for me.
O you know that I must say goodbye
O goodbye
Even though you will betray me
The very minute that I leave.

O say goodbye to the little girl tree
O Lord you know that I must say goodbye
To that little girl tree.
I rise up her girl-child lumps and slipping knots
Into her laden boughs,
And amongst her roping limbs
Like a swollen neck-vein branching
Into smaller lesser veins
That must all just sing and say goodbye,
And let her blossom veils fly
Her velvet gown
Down down down
Down down down

Down down down—and goodbye
For you know that I must say goodbye

To a rhythm softly tortured
Of a motion back and forth,
That's a rhythm sweetly tortured
O that's the rhythms of the orchard
And you know that I must say goodbye
To that little girl tree.
O goodbye. Yes goodbye.
For you know that I must die.
Down down down
Down down down
Down down down and goodbye.
For you know that I must die
Yes you know that I must die
O-o you know that I must die.

TRAIN LONG SUFFERING

Woo-woooooooooooo Woo!
In the name of pain!
   (In the name of pain and suffering)
In the name of pain!
   (In the name of pain and suffering)
There comes a train
   (There comes a train)
Yeah! A long black train
   (There comes a train)
Lord, a long black train.

Woo-woo! woo-woo!

Punched from the tunnel
   (The tunnel of love is long and lonely)
Engines steaming like a fist
   (A fistful of memories)
Into the jolly jaw of morning
   (Yeah! O yeah!)
O baby it gets smashed!
   (You know that it gets smashed)
O baby it gets smashed
   (You know that it gets smashed).

I kick every goddam splinter
Into all the looking eyes in the world,
Into all the laughing eyes
Of all the girls in the world
Ooooooo-woooooooh
She ain't never coming back
She ain't never coming back
She ain't never coming back
And the name of the pain is...
The name of the pain is...
The name of the pain is
A train long-suffering.

On rails of pain
   (On rails of pain and suffering)
There comes a train
   (There comes a train long-suffering)
On rails of pain
   (On rails of pain and suffering)
O baby blow its whistle in the rain.

Woo-oo Woo! Woo-woo Woo!

Who's the engine-driver?
   (The engine-driver's over yonder)
His name is Memory
   (Memory is his name)
O Memory is his name
   (Wooooooo-oo!)
Destination... Misery
   (Pain and misery)
O pain and misery
   (Pain and misery)
O pain and misery! Hey! Hey!
   (Pain and misery)
Hey! that's a sad looking sack!
Oooh that's a sad looking sack!
And the name of the pain is...
And the name of the pain is...
Oooh the name of the pain is...
A train long-suffering.

There is a train!
   (It's got a name)
Yeah! It's a train long-suffering
O Lord a train
   (A long black train)
Lord! Of pain and suffering
Each night so black
   (O yeah! So black)
And in the darkness of my sack
I'm missing you baby
   (I'm missing you)

And I just don't know what to do
  (Don't know what to do)
  (Train long-suffering, Train long-suffering).
Train long-suffering. Train long-suffering.
O she ain't never coming back
O she ain't never coming back
O she ain't never coming back
O she ain't never coming back
And the name of the pain is...
The name of the pain is...
The name of the train is...
The name of the train is
Pain and suffering.

BLACK CROW KING

Mmmmm Mmmmmm Mmmmm
I am the black crow king
Mmmmmmm Mmmmm Mmmmmmm
I am the black crow king
Keeper of the nodding corn
Bam! Bam! Bam! Bam!
All the hammers are a-talking
All the nails are a-singing
So sweet and low.

You can hear it in the valley
Where live the lame and the blind
They climb the hill out of its belly
They leave with mean black boots on.

'I just made a simple gesture
They jumped up and nailed it to my shadow
My gesture was a hooker
You know, my shadow's made of timber'.

And this storm is a-rolling
And this storm is a-rolling
All down on me.

And I'm still here rolling after everybody's gone
And I'm still here rolling after everybody's gone
I'm still here rolling and I'm left on my own
The blackbirds have all flown!
Everyone's rolled on!

I am the black crow king
Keeper of the trodden corn
I am the black crow king
I won't say it again.
And the rain it raineth daily, Lord
And wash away my clothes
I surrender up my arms
To a company of crows.

I am the black crow king
I won't say it again
And all the thorns are a-crowning king,
Ruby on each spine,
And the spears are a-sailing
O my o my.

And the storm is a-rolling
The storm is a-rolling
All down on me.

And I'm still here rolling after everybody's gone
I'm still here rolling after everybody's gone
I'm still here rolling and left on my own
Those blackbirds they have flown and I am on my own.

I am the black crow king
Keeper of the forgotten corn
The King! The King!
I'm the king of nothing at all.
The hammers are a-talking
The nails are a-singing
The thorns are a-crowning him
The spears are a-sailing
The crows are a-mocking
The corn is a-nodding
The storm is a-rolling
The storm is a-rolling
The storm is a-rolling down
The storm is a-rolling down
The storm is a-rolling
Down on me
Rolling down on me
Rolling down on me.

KNOCKIN' ON JOE

These chains of sorrow, they are heavy, it is true
And these locks cannot be broken, no, not with one thousand keys
O Jailor, you wear a ball-and-chain you cannot see
You can lay your burden on me
You can lay your burden down on me
You can lay your burden down upon me
But you cannot lay down those memories.

Woooo wooo wooo
Woooo wooo wooo
Here I go!
Knockin' on Joe!
This square foot of sky will be mine till I die
Knockin' on Joe.
Woooo wooo wooo
All down the row
Knockin' on Joe.

O Warden I surrender to you
Your fists can't hurt me anymore
You know, these hands will never wash
These dirty Death Row floors.
O Preacher, come closer, you don't scare me anymore
Just tell Nancy not to come here
Just tell her not to come here anymore
Tell Nancy not to come
And let me die in the memory of her arms.

O Wooo wooo wooo
Wooo wooo woooo
All down the row
Knockin' on Joe.
O you kings of halls and ends of halls
You will die within these walls
And I'll go, all down the row
Knockin' on Joe.

O Nancy's body is a coffin, she wears my tombstone at her head
O Nancy's body is a coffin, she wears my tombstone at her head
She wears her body like a coffin
She wears a dress of gold and red
She wears a dress of gold and red
She wears a dress of red and gold
Grave-looters at my coffin before my body's even cold.

It's a door for when I go
Knockin' on Joe.
These hands will never mop your dirty Death Row floors
No! You can hide! You can run!
O but your trial is yet to come
O you can run! You can hide!
But you have yet to be tried!
You can lay your burden down here
You can lay your burden down here
Knockin' on Joe
You can lay your burden upon me
You can lay your burden down upon me
Knockin' on Joe
You can't hurt me anymore
Knockin' on Joe.

WANTED MAN

I'm a wanted man
Wanted man
I'm wanted
I'm a wanted man
O yeah, O honey I'm a wanted man.

Wanted man in Arizona, wanted man in Galveston
Wanted man in El Dorado, this wanted man's in great demand.

If you ever catch me sleeping,
    and you see a price flash above my head,
Take a look again my friend, that's a gun pointing at your head.

Wanted man by the Borland sisters, wanted man by Kate Callaghan
Honey don't you try and tell me you don't want me
    'cause I'm a wanted man.
Wanted man who's lost his will to live,
    wanted man who won't lay down,
There's a woman kneeling at an unmarked grave
    pushing daisies in the ground.

Wanted man in the windy city, wanted man in Tennessee
Wanted man in Broken Arrow, wanted man in Wounded Knee
Wanted man in Jackson town, wanted man in El Paso
I've got bounties on my head in towns I would never think to go.

Wanted man in Arizona, wanted man in Louisville
Wanted man deep in Death Valley,
    wanted man up in the Hollywood hills.

If the Devil comes collecting,
    'cause heaven don't want no wanted man
He'd better wear a six-gun on his hip and hold another in his hand.

If you love a wanted man, you'd best hold him while you can
Because you're going to wake up one morning
    and find the man you wanted he is gone.

Wanted man in New York City, wanted man in San Antone
Wanted man down in Lorado, wanted man in Tupelo.

Wanted man in the state of Texas, wanted man in the state of Maine
This wanted man's in the state of leaving you baby,
    jumping on that midnight train.

Wanted man in every cat-house, wanted man in a million saloons
Wanted man is a ghost in a hundred houses,
    a shadow in a thousand rooms.

Wanted man down at St Louis, wanted man in New Orleans
Wanted man in Muscle Bay, wanted man in Cripple Creek
Wanted man in Detroit City, wanted man in San Antone
But there's one place I'm not wanted, Lord,
    it's the place that I call home.

O wanted man, wanted man
If the Devil comes collecting he'd better hold a six-gun in his hand.

BLIND LEMON JEFFERSON

Bline Lemon Jefferson is a-comin
Tap tap tappin with his cane
Bline Lemon Jefferson is a-comin
Tap tap tappin with his cane
His last ditch lies down the road of trials
Half filled with rain.

O sycamore, sycamore!
Stretch your arms across the storm
Down fly two greasy brother crows
They hop n bop n hop n bop hop on bop
Like the tax-man to come to call
They go knock knock! knock knock!
Hop n bop hop n bop
They slap a death-writ on his door.

Here come the Judgement train
Git on board!
And turn that big black engine home.
O let's roll! Let's roll!
Down the tunnel
The terrible tunnel of his world
Waiting at his final station
Like a bigger blacker third bird
O let's roll! Let's roll!

O his road is dark and lonely
He don't drive no Cadilac
O his road is dark and holy
He don't drive no Cadilac
If that sky serves as his eyes
Then that moon is a cataract.

Let's roll! Yeah let's roll!

NECROPOLIS HO!

vaudville

The night Hank blew into Necropolis

~~suffered by the ghost he had~~ ~~~~ given up ~~~~ back of his Pontiac

~~legend~~
~~myth~~ ~~looking like~~ ~~~~ ~~huckster~~ ~~who bummed~~ en

~~Slumped in~~ crumpled ~~~~ ~~crotchet~~ ~~quaver~~

burlesque
girl etc.   crotchet

His ~~~~ + story all ~~~~ up ~~done~~ ~~~~ the portion of his cup

~~collar~~
~~I relate~~ with hollow glory ~~~~   (sure)   ~~~~ a huckster in a ~~~~ suit ~~~~ fancy musical
(smooth)   suit

Sucking the stones of lonliness ~~~~ ~~~~ ~~of~~ every last lick
lozenge   till they ~~~~ were smooth * swallern   of flavour
a bitter ~~turn~~ that he would savour
in time ~~~~

spots

The last drop, ~~would mark the spot~~, whate the crotchet died a
                    like the   quaver
            ~~~~ crutch is always kicked from unner us

like ~~a~~ the sacks of woe piled atop of us

~~Heck could~~ a hump of trouble, O ~~bath of~~ ~~trands~~, O Necropolis Ho
I say *   * sack woe

A huckster slumped in the back of the Pontiac

THISTLES IN THE SOUL

THISTLES IN THE SOUL

The first time I saw Einsturzende Neubauten was on Dutch TV. It was the year 1982. The group I had back then—the Birthday Party—was doing a string of concerts in Holland, and it was toward the end of the tour—we were all near the brink of death. I was just making my way down the stairs of our humble but obliging hotel when an eerie, hypnotic sound came floating from the TV room, insidiously seductive, irresistably sad. To these baleful strains I found myself drawn, and as I stepped into the TV room all the notions of music that I held so precious were obliterated—in toto—by what I saw upon the screen.

There was a young man, wearing thick glasses, blowing into a bent drainpipe. Later I was informed that the name was Alexander von Borsig. The name of the young man, that is—not the drainpipe. The drainpipe was called the "Thirsty Animal". Thanks to the typically unorthodox, if not downright primitive Dutch camera-work, we were made to watch the manic von Borsig without interuption for all of five or six minutes, seeing his naturally pale teutonic complexion deepen with the passing seconds to that of a ripe plum. How lonely the cry of the Thirsty Animal seemed, its weird pule hanging in the air like a wheezing, dying siren. I remember von Borsig's face turn the exact colour of the red stockings worn by Heidi, the hotel maid. Hello.

Then a terrible rumbling, that seemed to come from the gut of a different beast—a hungry one—began to ravage the weeping-ground trodden by von Borsig's Thirsty Animal until the two were united in a sordid copulation of sound that hit me right in the dick. It was like Ulysses & his drunken sailors had jumped a lone siren, rolled her over & pack-raped her there on the rocks. And with a patience one seldom sees in this sort of TV music show, the camera moved across the stage and froze on a man holding two mallets, standing next to two large pieces of corrogated sheet-metal, which he bludgeoned louder and louder, while von Borsig kept blowing—working on a brain tumour. This man was Endruh Unruh, complete with Hitler-moustache and a head like a battlefield. Finally, the camera found the third man. He was the most beautiful man in the world. He stood there in a black leotard and black rubber pants, black rubber boots. Around his neck hung a thoroughly fucked guitar. His skin cleared to his bones, his skull was an utter disaster, scabbed and hacked, and his eyes bulged out of their orbits like a blind man's. And yet, the eyes stared at us as if to herald some divine visitation. Here stood a man on the trashold of greatness; here stood a Napoleon victorious amongst his spoils, a conquering Caesar parading his troops, a Christ akimbo on Calvary. Blixa Bargeld.

For sixty seconds, this man stood as if paralysed, hexed by his own madness. Then he opened his mouth and let out a scream that sounded like somebody was pulling a thistle out of his soul.

After the TV show, a friend of mine told me he had met Susanna Kunke—of Malaria—in Amsterdam the day before, and she had told him about a party with E.N. in an Amsterdam hotel. They had all been naked—mucking about. Alexander von Borsig had sat in a corner, staring at a metronome and rocking back and forth—tock tock tock tock tock—to its rhythm.

A few months later, after the Birthday Party had moved from London to Berlin, we got to know E.N. and became friends. I remember visiting them while they were recording "Thirsty Animal" in a small Kreuzberg studio; the studio was cold and fusty and full of amps, trash and steel. And in the middle of the room a microphone pointed to a small, mangy dog rooting around in a steaming pile of pig guts. Blixa Bargeld had a contact-mike taped to his chest, while the musclebound Mufti beat on this natural soundingboard with his fists. Boom-Boom Boom-Boom. Boom-Boom Boom-Boom. E.N. belong to that mass of bands that operate in the nebulous area of "Innovative Music", which, to me, is a title applied much too quickly and much too generously. And which is all too readily embraced by so many groups these days, particularly in Germany; groups whose ambitions have no other end than their own meaningless self-perpetuation through the intimidation of the unknown, the new. Not so Einsturzende Neubauten. They are simply a "great" band—and I use the word in the classical sense. To me, the essence of their greatness does not lie in their unorthodox attitude toward making music—rather it is based on a fundamentally orthodox premise. What makes E.N. great in my eyes is the same thing that makes Johnny Cash—or the Velvet Underground, John Lee Hooker, Suicide, Elvis, Dylan, Leadbelly, The Stooges—great. They are all innovators but what sets Hank Williams apart from the bulk of his contemporaries is the same thing that sets E.N. apart from the huge, faceless morass that modern New Wave music has become. Through their own hard work, by steadfast lack of compromise, through the pain of true self-expression, through a genuine love of their medium, they have attained a sound which is first authentic, and which is utterly their own. But not for the sole purpose of being different. They are a group which has developed its own special language for one reason—to give voice to their souls.

And this is the fundamental difference between E.N. and those who imitate them. This is why E.N. will remain timeless. They have always known the meaning and purpose of their medium: to give vent to the expression of the soul.

(A fan)

YOUR FUNERAL, MY TRIAL

Crow Jane

Sad Waters
The Carny
Your Funeral, My Trial
Jack's Shadow
Hard on for Love
She Fell Away

God's Hotel

The Mercy Seat

CROW JANE

O Cro-o-o-o-o-ow Jane
O Cro-o-o-o-o-ow Jane
Horrors in her head
Tongue dare not name
Lived by the river
The rollin' rivers of pain.

One shining eye on a hard-hat
Company close down the mine
Winking on the water they came
Twenny hard-hats, twenny eyes
In her damp clapboard shack
Just six foot by five
Killed all her whiskey
Poured their pistols dry.

O Cro-o-o-o-o-ow Jane
O Cro-o-o-o-o-ow Jane
Seems you've remembered
How to sleep, how to sleep
The yard-dogs in your turnips
The barn-dogs in the peat.

'O Mr. Smith and Mr. Wessen
Why you close up shop so late?'
'Just fitted out a gal who looked like a bird
Measured .32, .44, .38.
Asked that gal which road she was taking
Said she was walkin the road of hate'.
But she hopped a coal-trolley up to New Haven
Population: forty-eight.

O Cro-o-o-o-o-ow Jane
O Cro-o-o-o-o-ow Jane
Your guns are drunk and crying
They have followed you to your gate
That laughing home-stride back from New Haven
Population: twenny-eight.

SAD WATERS ~~Allan~~ ~~Hot~~ 11-01-1984

Down the road I walk with my sweet MARY
~~Lip~~ Hair of Gold + Lips like Cherries
To the River, where the Willows weep
~~Sat down~~ Took a ~~large~~ NAKED Root for a Loverseat

that rose out of the eaten soil
~~that bound to the~~ by creeping ivy coils
O Mary
and I don't know right from wrong You have seduced my soul
I am forever a ~~HOSTAGE~~ of your childs world
+ then I ran my tin cup heart along the prison
Of her ribs
+ giggling free, she waded in
She will never be mine
+ plaited all the willow vines rolling her all about her knee
Mary in the shallows, ~~where the carp dart~~
Laughing where (laughing) the carp dart
Spooked by the ~~new~~ shadow that she casts
.... lets ~~Hit cross~~

SAD WATERS

Down the road I look and there runs Mary
Hair of gold and lips like cherries.
We go down to the river where the willows weep,
Take a naked root for a lovers' seat
That rose out of the bitten soil,
But bound to the ground by creeping ivy coils.
O Mary you have seduced my soul
(And I don't know right from wrong)
Forever a hostage of your child's world.

And then I ran my tin-cup heart along
The prison of her ribs,
And with a toss of her curls
That little girl goes wading in,
Rolling her dress up past her knee
Turning these waters into wine
Then she plaited all the willow vines.

Mary in the shallows laughing
Over where the carp dart
Spooked by the new shadows that she cast
Across these sad waters and across my heart.

THESE SAD WATERS by Nick Cave

2x [Lord, I'm still ~~sittin~~ here, sittin
Yeah, Mary, she is still, across the sea.
Lord, I believe in a ~~Greater~~ Plan,
Yes, I do.
I believe, Lord, in a Greater Plan
and I know I'm being tested, O I know
I am
and I know that there was a reason
O yes, a ~~Greater~~ Reason, a ~~Greater~~ Plan
that Mary was taken from my hands
across the ocean, into another ~~arms~~
O The years, Lord, they go by.
Lord, the years are long
O I'm still sittin here + ~~thinkin long~~
Lord, I know them years, th~~   grain~~
O a grain
Part of your Greater Plan
that I wait + sit + wait, O Lord
sit + wait to understand
I think long + its hard + long, Lord, are the years
O I stand + I walk to the window, push the
O these Grains of Sand are killin me / shutters out
I push the Shutters out + ~~took way across th~~
way down upon this Great black City

O Lord, the people look like ANTS
From way up here
All This Thinkin is Killin me, ~~Lord~~
I think of You, Lord knows I ~~do~~ try
And I think of them + her harp partin
+ I think of "FOREVER" When she laughs
Lord I think of "ETERNITY" + closing when she LIES
I think of "NEVER" * CLOSING WHEN SHE CM
Lookin' down, Way Up + thinkin at this window.

I remember ~~And~~ Mary, In the shallows.
Laughing.
Plaiting at the Willow vines
Over ~~where the~~ Carp dart
Spooked by her new shadow cast
across these Sad Waters. Lord, like a cloud
and across ~~the~~ Heart.
and across my Heart.

—— END ——

THE CARNY   by Nick Cave 1986

BCDPGHIKLMNPQRSTVWZ
A

① AND NO-ONE SAW THE CARNY GO
AND THE WEEKS FLEW BY
UNTIL ~~FINALY~~ THEY MOVED ON THE SHOW
LEAVING HIS CARAVAN BEHIND
IT WAS PARKED OUT ON THE SOUTH EAST RIDGE
AND AS THE COMPANY CROSSED THE BRIDGE
WITH THE FIRST RAIN FILLING THE BONE'DRY RIVER BED
IT SHONE, JUST SO, UPON THE EDGE

② GOLIATH; MANDRAKE;
~~THE~~ tMDRAKE, THE ~~KNUTFORD~~; ~~GOLIATH~~ t THE GEEKS t THE HIRED HANDS
he was not one among them who did not caste ~~on~~ ~~AND EVEN AS THEY CROSSED THE VALLEY~~
in the hope, the Carny, would, at ~~long~~ ~~last~~ ✓
~~within grow~~ ~~soul~~ ~~a puzzle to bumbs ahead,~~ ~~return~~ ✓
for his own kind

w/ his medicine bag t his Tome No.9

" AWAY AWAY...WE'RE SAD TO SAY "
↑ THERE WAS NOT ONE AMONG THEM THAT DID NOT CAST AN EYE ∃
↓ MANDRAKE, ~~THE KNUTFORD~~, goliath,   BEHIND ∠
A1   t the GEEKS t
The HIRED HANDS
IN THE HOPE THAT THE CARNY, ~~MAY AT LAST APPEAR~~
WOULD ARRIVE IN TIME
FOR THINGS ~~THAT~~ WERE JUST NOT THE SAME
~~AND STILL THE CARNY DID NOT SHOW~~

③ AND THE CARNY HAD A HORSE, ALL SKIN t BONE
. BOW-BACKED NAG, THAT HE NAMED SORROW
~~ow IT WAS BURIED IN A SHALLOW GRAVE~~ ~~Bony~~
ow IT WAS BURIED IN A SHALLOW GRAVE
IN THE THEN PARCHED MEADOW

HAD A HORSE, OF SKIN t BONE
AND THE CARNY'S ~~PONY~~ ~~GEL~~ ~~WERE~~ ~~HORSE~~
BOW BACKED NAG THAT HE NAME SORROW
AN' ~~BROKEN~~ NAG NAMED SORROW
WAS BURIED IN A SHALLOW GRAVE
IN THE THEN PARCHED MEADOW

AND THE DWARVES WERE GIVEN THE TASK OF DIGGING THE DITCH
PART
AND LAYING THE ~~WRETCHED~~ CARCASS IN THE GROUND
BEAST
AND BOSS BELLINI, WAVING HIS SMOKING PISTOL ROUND
SAYING, "THE NAG WAS DEAD ~~NEIGHT~~ MEAT!
WE CAINT AFFORD TO CARRY DEAD WEIGHT" X ?
THE WHOLE COMPANY STANDING ~~AROUND~~ ~~LOOKING~~ ABOUT, ~~NOT~~
ABOUT
~~HEADS~~ ~~INCLINED~~. NOT MAKING A SOUND
AND TURNING TO THE ~~GROUP OF~~ DWARVES PERCHED ON THE
THE
GATE & BOSS
ENCLOSURE ~~WALL~~ ~~HE~~ SAID, "~~QUIT YA MUSIC AND~~
"BURY THIS LUMP OF OF CROW BAIT"
~~AND BEFORE THEY'D PATTED FLAT THE MOUND~~
~~THE HEAVENS GROWLED AND OPENED UP~~
~~AND THE RAIN CAME HAMMERIN DOWN~~
~~AND THE RAIN CAME HAMMERIN DOWN~~

BUT Before ~~they~~ COULD PAT FLAT THE MOUND ~~UP~~ t THE MOUND
The H~~ ~~ The rain came hammering down

THE CARNY

And no-one saw the carny go
And the weeks flew by
Until they moved on the show,
Leaving his caravan behind.
It was parked up on the south-east ridge
And as the company crossed the bridge
With the first rain filling the bone-dry river bed
It shone, just so, upon the edge.

Dog-boy, Atlas, Half-man, The Geeks, the hired hands,
There was not one among them that did not cast an eye behind
In the hope that the carny would return to his own kind.

And the carny had a horse, all skin and bone,
A bow-backed nag that he named Sorrow.
Now it is buried in a shallow grave
In the then parched meadow.

And the dwarves were given the task of digging the ditch
And laying the nag's carcass in the ground,
And Boss Bellini, waving his smoking pistol around
Saying 'The nag is dead meat
We can't afford to carry dead weight'.
The whole company standing about
Not making a sound,
And turning to the dwarves perched on the enclosure gate
The Boss says 'Bury this lump of crow bait'.

And then the rain came hammering down
Everybody running for their wagons
Tying all the canvass flaps down.
The mangy cats growling in their cages.
The Bird-Girl flapping and squawking around.

The whole valley reeking of wet beast,
Wet beast and rotten hay,
Freak and brute creation
Packed up and on their way.

The three dwarves peering from their wagon's hind,
Moses says to Noah 'We shoulda dugga deepa one',
Their grizzled faces like dying moons
Still dirty from the digging done.

And as the company passed from the valley
Into higher ground
The rain beat on the ridge and on the meadow
And on the mound
Until nothing was left, nothing at all
Except the body of Sorrow
That rose in time
To float upon the surface of the eaten soil.

And a murder of crows did circle round
First one, then the others flapping blackly down.

And the carny's van still sat upon the edge
Tilting slowly as the firm ground turned to sludge.

And the rain it hammered down.

And no-one saw the carny go
I say it's funny how things go.

HE 3 DWARVES PEERING FROM THEIR WAGONS HIND   *AWAY AWAY..*

MOSES SAYS TO NOAH. "THE CARNY AINT GUNNA SHOW UP"   ~~ALL~~ *AND THE RAIN CAME HAMMERING DOWN*

~~*SHOULD'VE*~~   ~~THE WHOLE COMPANY~~ RUNNING FOR THEIR WAGONS

WE OUGHTA DUGGER DEEPER, ~~SHOULD DUG EM~~ *ONE.* ~~EVERY BODY CRIED~~ ~~TO A THE,~~

THEIR GRISSLED FACES, LIKE 3 DYING MOONS   TYING ALL THE CANVAS FLAPS ~~FLAPS~~ DOWN

STILL DIRTY FROM THEIR DIGGING DONE   THE MANGY CATS GROWLING IN THEIR CAGES

                                                       THE BIRD-GIRL FLAPPING AND SQUAWKING IN THE ROUND

                                                       IN ~~THE WORDS~~ THE WHOLE VALLEY REEKING OF WET BEAST

                                                       WET BEAST AND ROTTEN SODDEN HAY

                                                                                   ALL
                                                       FREAK AND BRUTE CREATION PACKED UP

                                                       AND ON THEIR WAY,

DWARF MOSES SAID TO

MOSES ~~AND CHARLIE THE DWARF~~ *SAID TO DWARF NOAH*   AND THE DWARVES ~~SHUFFLING~~   *MOSES SAID TO NOAH*

"AH GUESS DE CARNY AINT GUNNA SHOW   ~~ALWAYS FIRST WITH A CROW TO PLUCK~~ *"THE CARNY AINT GUNNA SHOW"*

WISHING THEY'D DONE A BETTER J OF BURIN *SORROW*   *+ KITTLE* *"WE OUGHTA HAVE DUG 'IM DEEPER*

MOSES   ~~NOAH~~   WERE STRANGELY ~~SOBERED~~ BY THE GOING   *OR WE SHOULD DUG EM DEEPER*

OLD MOSES SAYING TO ~~NOAH~~ *& MOSES*   THEIR GRISLED FACES PEERING FROM THE WAGONS HIND

"AH GUESS DE CARNY AINT GUNNA SHOW UP   LIKE THREE DYING MOONS   *THE WINDOW OF THE TINY VAN*

AND NOAH SAYING "WE OUGHTA HAVE DUG HIM DEEPER   *THEIR*

                                                       STILL ~~DIRTY~~ FROM THE DIGGING DONE

                                                           DIRTY

                                                       AND CHARLIE, THE ELDEST OF THE THREE SAYING

                                                       "AH GUESS DE CARNY AINT GUNNA SHOW"

                                                       AND THEY WERE SILENT FOR A SPELL

                                                       WISHING THEY'D DONE A BETTER JOB OF BURING SORROW

                                                                     FROM THE VALLEY

                                                    X AND AS THE COMPANY PASSED INTO HIGHER GROUND

                                                       THE RAIN BEAT ON THE RIDGE, AND ON THE MEADOW, AND ON THE

                                                       UNTIL NOTHING WAS LEFT, *NOTHING LEFT AT ALL*   MOUND.

AND THE COMPANY PASSED FROM THE VALLEY   ~~OF NOTHING~~

INTO "HIGHER GROUND   EXCEPT ~~CORPSE~~ OF ~~THIS~~ SORROW ~~SO~~ THAT ROSE ?

& RUNNING FOR   IN TIME, TO ~~THE SURFACE~~ OF THE EATEN SOIL

'CEPT THE BODY OF SORROW   *FLOAT OPEN SURFACE*

THAT ROSE IN TIME

TO FLOAT UPON THE SURFACE   AND A MURDER OF CROWS DID CIRCLE ROUND

OF THE EATEN SOIL   FIRST ONE? AND THEN THE OTHERS FLAPPING BLACKLY DOWN

                                                       AND THE CARNY'S VAN STILL SAT UPON THE EDGE

                                                    ✓ TILTING SLOWLY AS THE FIRM GROUND TURNED TO SLUDGE

                                                       AN THE RAIN IT HAMMERED DOWN

                                                    X   AN THE RAIN IT HAMMERED DOWN

                                                       NO ONE SAW THE CARNY GO

                                                       I SAY IT FUNNY HOW ~~THE~~ *GO*

                                                                          THINGS

Your Funeral, my trial   by Nick Cave

words & music

Verse 1

I am a crooked man
and I've walked a crooked mile
Night, the shameless widow
doffed her weeds, in a pile
The stars all winked at me
They shamed a child
Your funeral, my trial.

Verse 2

A thousand Marys lured me
to feathered beds and fields of clover
Bird with crooked wing cast
its wicked shadow over
A bauble moon did mock
and trinket stars did smile
Your funeral, my trial

Verse 3

Here I am, little lamb...
Let all the bells in whoredom ring
All the crooked bitches that she was
(Mongers of Pain)
Saw the moon
Become a fang
Your funeral, my trial

YOUR FUNERAL, MY TRIAL

I am a crooked man
And I've walked a crooked mile.
Night, the shameless widow
Doffed her weeds, in a pile.
The stars all winked at me
They shamed a child
Your funeral, my trial.

A thousand Marys lured me
To feathered beds and fields of clover,
Bird with crooked wing cast
It's wicked shadow over.
A bauble moon did mock
And trinket stars did smile.
Your funeral, my trial.

Here I am, little lamb...
Let all the bells in whoredom ring.
All the crooked bitches that she was
(Mongers of pain)
Saw the moon
Become a fang.
Your funeral, my trial.

JAN 1986

I AM A CROOKED MAN
AND I'VE WALKED A CROOKED MILE
BENEATH THIS HUMP OF TROUBLES, SIR
I'VE CLIMBED MANY A STILE
THE MOON WAS LIKE A GILDED HORN
WITHIN A MAIDEN'S MIDNIGHT GOWN
IN A FOREST DARK WITH WHISPERING
I LAY MY TROUBLES DOWN
DEMENTIA, SIR, I DO NOT KNOW
NOR SLEEPS DIM PREMISE DID   ENTICE
BUT LIKE A MOB OF CRUCIFIX S, SIR
THE TREES CAME LOOKING FOR A CHRIST
THEIR TRUNKS WERE CLAD IN SEQUINED GOWNS
WITH CHEAP TRINKETS EVERY PLACE
THEIR PAINTED NAILS WERE DRIVEN ~~THROUGH~~

~~EMBRACE~~
OUR BROKE OAKEN EMBRACE   OUR
I RECALL, DEAR SIR, THEIR PROMISES
~~THEIR FOANS, THEIR SCENTED CRIES~~
THE PRINETIMES SCENTED CRIES
BUT IN THE WINTER OF THESE EVER-DEADS
~~DID BURGEON~~ I LEARNED OF THEIR DEVICE

unfinished

lies lies lies

JACK'S SHADOW

They dragged Jack and his shadow
From the hole
And the bulb that burned above him
Did shine both day and night
And his shadow learned to love his
Little darks and greater light
And the sun it shined
And the sun it shined
And the sun it shined
A little stronger.

Jack wept and kissed his shadow
'Goodbye'.
Spat from the dirty dungeons
Into a truly different din,
Shat from their institutions
Into a fully different din.
And his shadow soon became a wife
And children plagued his latter life
Until one night he took a skinning knife
And stole into the town
And tracked his shadow down.

Said that shadow to Jack Henry
'What's wrong?'
Jack said 'A home is not a hole
And shadow you're just a gallow that I hang my body from,
O shadow you're a shackle from which my time is never done'.
Then he peeled his shadow off in strips,
He peeled his shadow off in strips
Then he kneeled his shadow on some steps
And cried 'what have I done?'

And the sun it shined
And the sun it shined
I say 'Love is blind'
And is it any wonder?
Is it any wonder?'

Jack and his damned shadow
Is gone.
And though each one of us are want to duly mourn
And though each one of us are want to duly mourn
'Tis done in brighter corners now
'Tis done in brighter corners now
Now that Jack's black shadow's gone.

And the sun it shines
And the sun it shines
And the sun it shines
A little stronger.

I swear, love is blind
Oooh love is blind
Yeah love is blind
And is it any wonder?

'Tis done in brighter corners now
'Tis done in brighter corners now
Now that Jack's black shadow's gone.

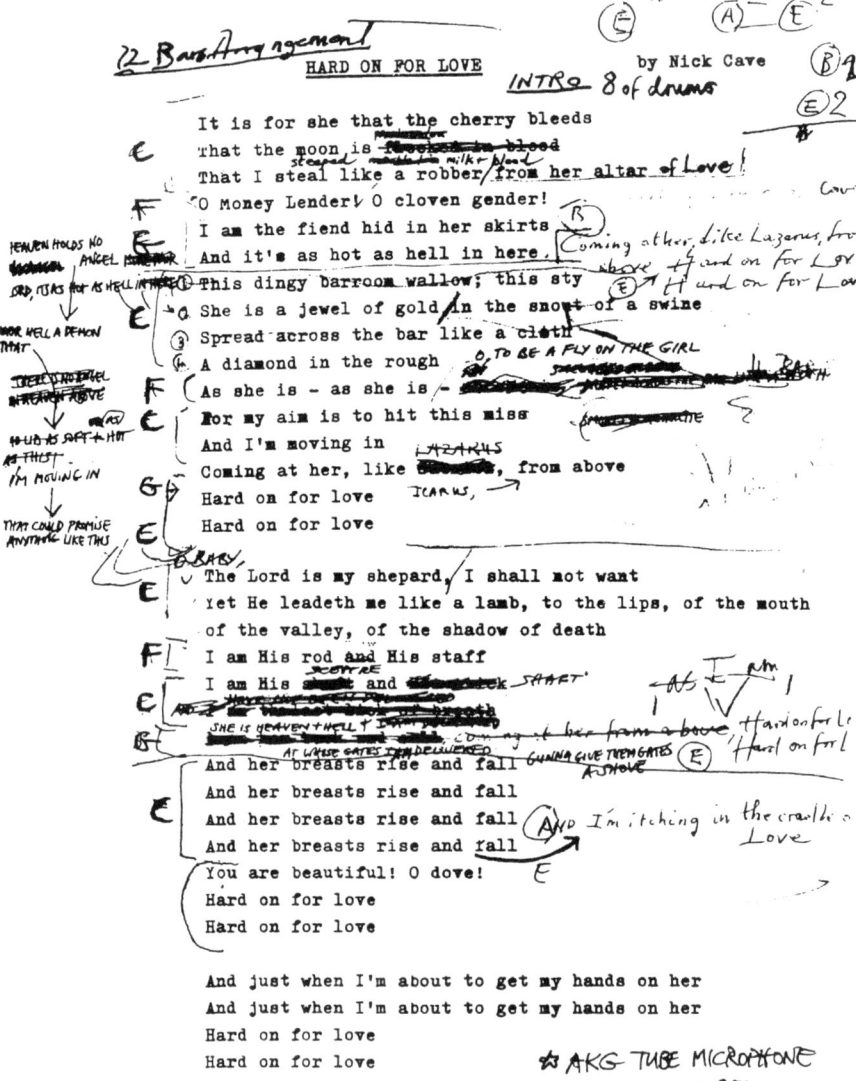

12 Bars Arrangement

HARD ON FOR LOVE   by Nick Cave

INTRO 8 of drums

E^4 A^2 E^2
B^2
E^2

It is for she that the cherry bleeds
That the moon is steeped in milk + blood
That I steal like a robber/from her altar of Love!
O Money Lender! O cloven gender!
I am the fiend hid in her skirts
And it's as hot as hell in here.   Coming other, like Lazarus, from above   Hard on for Love
This dingy barroom wallow; this sty   Hard on for Love
She is a jewel of gold in the snout of a swine
Spread across the bar like a cloth
A diamond in the rough   O, TO BE A FLY ON THE GIRL
As she is - as she is -
For my aim is to hit this miss
And I'm moving in   LAZARUS
Coming at her, like Icarus, from above
Hard on for love
Hard on for love

HEAVEN HOLDS NO ANGEL
LORD, IT'S AS HOT AS HELL IN HERE
NOR HELL A DEMON THAT
THERE'S NO DEVIL IN HEAVEN ABOVE
HELL IS SOFT + HOT AS THIS?
I'M MOVING IN
THAT COULD PROMISE ANYTHING LIKE THIS

O BABY

The Lord is my shepard, I shall not want
Yet He leadeth me like a lamb, to the lips, of the mouth
of the valley, of the shadow of death
I am His rod and His staff   SCEPTRE
I am His shot and SHAFT
SHE IS HEAVEN + HELL + ...   AS I AM
AT WHOSE GATES I'M DELIVERED   GUNNA GIVE THEM GATES   Hard on for Lo
And her breasts rise and fall   ABOVE   (E)   Hard on for Lo
And her breasts rise and fall
And her breasts rise and fall   AND I'm itching in the cradle o
And her breasts rise and fall   Love
You are beautiful! O dove!   E
Hard on for love
Hard on for love

And just when I'm about to get my hands on her
And just when I'm about to get my hands on her
Hard on for love
Hard on for love   ☆ AKG TUBE MICROPHONE
                   ☆ NEUMANN U67

--end--

HARD ON FOR LOVE

It is for she that the cherry bleeds
That the moon is steeped in milk and blood
That I steal like a robber
From her alter of love.
O money lender! O cloven gender!
I am the fiend hid in her skirts
And it's as hot as hell in here
Coming at her as I am from above
Hard on for love. Hard on for love.
Hard on for love. Hard on for love.

Well, I swear I seen that girl before
Like she walked straight outa the book of Leviticus
But they can stone me with stones I don't care
Just as long as I can get to kiss
Those gypsy lips! Gypsy lips!
My aim is to hit this miss
And I'm movin in (I'm moving in)
Comin at her like Lazarus from above
Hard on lor love. Hard on for love.
Hard on for love. Hard on for love.

The Lord is my shepherd I shall not want
The Lord is my shepherd I shall not want
But he leadeth me like a lamb to the lips
Of the mouth of the valley of the shadow of death.
I am his rod and his staff
I am his sceptre and shaft
And she is Heaven and Hell
At whose gates I ain't been delivered.
I'm gunna give them gates a shove.
Hard on for love. Hard on for love.
Hard on lor love. Hard on for love.

And her breasts rise and fall
Her breast rise and fall
Her breast rise and fall
Her breast rise and fall

And just when I'm about to get my hands on her
Just when I'm about to get my hands on her
Just when I'm about to get my hands on her
Just when I'm about to get my hands on her
You are beautiful! O dove!
Hard on for love. Hard on for love.
Hard on for love. Hard on for love.

Just when I'm about to get my hands on her
Just when I'm about to get my hands on her

Her breasts rise and fall
Her breasts rise and fall

Just when I'm about to get my hands on her
Just when I'm about to get my hands on her

Hard on for love. Hard on for love.
Hard on for love. Hard on for love.

SHE FELL AWAY

Once she lay open like a road
Carved apart the madness that I stumbled from
But she fell away
She fell away
Shed me like a skin
She fell away
Left me holding everything.

Once the road lay open like a girl
And we drank and laughed and threw the bottle over.
But she fell away
She fell away
I did not see the cracks form
As I knelt to pray
I did not see the crevice yawn, no.

Sometimes
At night I feel the end it is at hand
My pistol going crazy in my hand
For she fell away
O she fell away
Walked me to the brink
Then fell away
I did not see her fall
To better days
Sometimes I wonder was she ever there at all.
She fell away
She fell away
She fell away.

GOD'S HOTEL

Everybody got a room
Everybody got a room
Everybody got a room
In God's Hotel.
Everybody got a room.
Well you'll never see a sign hangin on the door
Sayin 'No vacancies here anymore'.

Everybody got wings
Everybody got wings
Everybody got wings
In God's Hotel.
Everybody got wings.
You'll never see a sign hangin on the door
Sayin 'At no time may both feet leave the floor'.

Everybody got a harp
Everybody got a harp
Everybody got a harp
In God's Hotel.
Everybody has got a harp.
You'll never see a sign hangin on the wall
Sayin 'No harps allowed in the hotel *at all*'.

Everybody got a cloud
Everybody got a cloud
Everybody got a cloud
In God's Hotel.
Everybody got a cloud.
Well you'll never see a sign hangin in the hall
Sayin 'Smoking and drinking will be thy downfall'.

Everybody holds a hand
Everybody holds a hand
Everybody holds a hand
In God's Hotel.
Everybody holds a hand.
You'll never see a sign hung up above your door
'No visitors allowed in rooms, *By Law!*'

Everybody's halo shines
Everybody's halo shines
Everybody's halo shines
In God's Hotel.
Everybody's halo lookin fine.
You won't see a sign staring at you from the wall
Sayin 'Lights Out! No burnin the midnight oil!'

Everybody got credit
Everybody got credit
Everybody got credit
In God's Hotel.
Everybody got good credit.
You'll never see a sign stuck on the cash-box drawer
Sayin 'Credit Tomorrow!!' or 'Want Credit?!? Haw, haw haw!!'

Everybody is blind
Everybody is blind
Everybody is blind
In God's Hotel.
Everybody is blind.
You'll never see a sign on the front door
'No red-skins. No Blacks. And that means you, baw!'

Everybody is deaf
Everybody is deaf
Everybody is deaf
In God's Hotel.
Everybody is deaf.
You'll never find a sign peeling off the bar-room wall
'Though shalt not blaspheme, cuss, holler or bawl'.

Everybody is dumb
Everybody is dumb
Everybody is dumb
In God's Hotel.
Everybody is dumb.
So you'll never see on the visiting-room wall
'Though shalt not blaspheme, cuss, holler or bawl'.

Everybody got Heaven
Everybody got Heaven
Everybody got Heaven
In God's Hotel.
Everybody got Heaven.
So you'll never see scribbled on the bathroom wall
'Let Rosy get ya Heaven, dial 686-844!'

THE MERCY SEAT

It began when they come took me from my home
And put me here in Dead Row,
Of which I am nearly wholly innocent, you know.
And I'll say it again
I… am… not… afraid… to… die.

I began to warm and chill
To objects and their fields,
A ragged cup, a twisted mop
The face of Jesus in my soup
Those sinister dinner meals
The meal trolley's wicked wheels
A hooked bone rising from my food
All things either good or ungood.

And the mercy seat is waiting
And I think my head is burning
And in a way I'm yearning
To be done with all this measuring of truth.
An eye for an eye A tooth for a tooth
And anyway I told the truth
And I'm not afraid to die.

Interpret signs and catalogue
A blackened tooth, a scarlet fog.
The walls are bad. Black. Bottom kind.
They are the sick breath at my hind
They are the sick breath at my hind
They are the sick breath at my hind
They are the sick breath gathering at my hind.

I hear stories from the chamber
How Christ was born into a manger
And like some ragged stranger
Died upon the cross.
And might I say it seems so fitting in its way
He was a carpenter by trade
Or at least that's what I'm told.

My good hand tatooed E.V.I.L.
Across its brother's fist
That filthy five! They did nothing to challenge or resist.

In Heaven His throne is made of gold
The ark of His testament is stowed
A throne from which I'm told
All history does unfold.
Down here it's made of wood and wire
And my body is on fire
And God is never far away.

Into the mercy seat I climb
My head is shaved, my head is wired
And like a moth that tries
To enter the bright eye
I go shuffling out of life
Just to hide in death awhile
And anyway I never lied.

My kill-hand is called E.V.I.L.
Wears a wedding band that's G.O.O.D.
'Tis a long-suffering shackle
Collaring all that rebel blood.

And the mercy seat is waiting
And I think my head is burning
And in a way I'm yearning
To be done with all this measuring of truth.
An eye for an eye
And a tooth for a tooth
And anyway I told the truth
And I'm not afraid to die.

And the mercy seat is burning
And I think my head is glowing
And in a way I'm hoping
To be done with all this weighing up of truth.
An eye for an eye
And a tooth for a tooth
And I've got nothing left to lose
And I'm not afraid to die.

And the mercy seat is glowing
And I think my head is smoking
And in a way I'm hoping
To be done with all these looks of disbelief.
An eye for an eye
And a tooth for a tooth
And anyway there was no proof
Nor a motive why.

And the mercy seat is smoking
And I think my head is melting
And in a way I'm helping
To be done with all this twisting of the truth.
A lie for a lie
And a truth for a truth
And I've got nothing left to lose
And I'm not afraid to die.

And the mercy seat is melting
And I think my blood is boiling
And in a way I'm spoiling
All the fun with all this truth and consequence.
And an eye for an eye
And a truth for a truth
And anyway I told the truth
And I'm not afraid to die.

And the mercy seat is waiting
And I think my head is burning
And in a way I'm yearning
To be done with all this measuring of proof.

And a life for a life
And a truth for a truth
And anyway I told the truth
But I'm not afraid to tell a lie.

And the mercy seat is waiting
And I think my head is burning
And in a way I'm yearning
To be done with all this measuring of truth.

An eye for an eye
And a truth for a truth
And anyway I told the truth
But I'm afraid I told a lie.

Index

Song titles are in **BOLD** type; Plays are in *ITALICS*; Prose pieces are in PLAIN type.

A

AMERICAN – SPEEDWAY – FEVER – TRASH 63

B

BIG – JESUS – TRASH – CAN 19
BLACK CROW KING 120
BLACK PEARL, THE 79
BLIND LEMON JEFFERSON 126
BLINE LEMON JEFFERSON **104**
BOX FOR BLACK PAUL, A 92

C

CABIN FEVER! 83
CARNY, THE 141
CHOP, THE 74
CROW JANE 135
CRY 9

D

DEAD JOE 25
DEAD SONG, A 13
DEEP IN THE WOODS 34
DIALOGUE WITH THE BAPTIST 71
DUMB EUROPE 40

E

EMERGENCY WARD 11:45 P.M. **58**

F

FEARS OF GUN 33
FIGURE OF FUN 11
FIVE FOOLS, THE 55
FROM HER TO ETERNITY 85

G

GARBAGE HEARTS **60**
GOD'S HOTEL 154
GOLDEN–HORN–HOOLIGAN 61

R

S

T

V

W

Y

Z